MW00967327

The Prince of Coincidence

Dave McGill

UNITED WRITERS PRESS, INC.
TUCKER, GEORGIA

Thank you!
Dave McGill

United Writers Press, Inc.
P.O. Box 326
Tucker, Georgia 30085-0326
1-866-857-4678

© 2006 David J. McGill
All Rights Reserved

ISBN-13: 978-0-9760824-8-4
ISBN: 0-9760824-8-9

Library of Congress Control Number: 2005911322

Printed in the United States of America

Cover Design by United Writers Press
Photograph courtesy of the author.

To Ancil Braning and J.E. "Jay" Crow
Friends Forever

TABLE OF CONTENTS

Introduction

This book is a collection of stories about events in my life. I am thankful for the friends and relatives I have known, especially those who appear in the stories and thus made them possible. In a few instances in which the tales might cause them embarrassment, I've changed their names.

The title story in the collection is about coincidences. As it happens, the book itself is yet another coincidence, as you'll see below.

I've been writing my stories for 32 years. All told, there are about three times as many as appear herein, but we had to start somewhere. I originally thought I would someday put the tales into a book, run a few copies at Kinko's, and give one to anybody who's in it.

But more recently, I decided that a better use of the stories might be to use them to raise money for a charity. This would require "real" publication, so I visited Vally Sharpe of United Writers Press, just three miles from my home, and we discussed the publication of a book comprising some of the tales. Vally asked me what the charity was going to be, and I replied that I hadn't yet come up with just the right one. Hurricane Katrina was to provide me with the answer.

The fury of that storm had devastated large sections of my home town of Slidell, Louisiana a couple of months earlier, destroying the church—Our Lady of Lourdes—in the parish where my family had worshipped in the 40s and 50s when I was growing up.

Here is the coincidence: The day after my meeting with Vally, I ran into Steve Lane, a friend at my current parish in Atlanta (Holy Cross), who had some interesting and timely news: "Dave, the parish council has approved my proposal that Holy Cross adopt as a sister parish Our Lady of Lourdes in Slidell, Louisiana, which was destroyed by Hurricane Katrina. We're going to help them rebuild. Aren't you from somewhere in Louisiana?"

Bingo. I had found my charity.

Besides Vally and Steve, I would also like to thank Carolyn, my wife of many talents, for her excellent proofreading and suggestions, and Kevin Lim for invaluable computer assistance. Finally, I'm grateful to *you* for buying the book and thereby contributing to the rebuilding of Our Lady of Lourdes in Slidell.

The Prince of Coincidence

The Bike That Was Ahead of Its Time

I remember my very best Christmas. I wish I could say it was 1945, but, alas, it was 1974. That year, in part because of the ages of our kids, we made perhaps our most successful effort to stress the meaning of the holiday as Jesus' birthday.

But the gifts were also special that year. My son and oldest daughter got 5-speed bicycles from Santa Claus. Gayle rode hers all day, between rain showers. We had to pry her off it at supper time, and I was reminded of a Christmas long before, when I was a child.

I was sick most of that December of 1945, and I can remember my mother going out to the shed off and on during the day to work on something; she wouldn't tell me what, saying only, "You'll have to wait till Christmas morning!" I knew they were building something, because World War II had just ended and we'd been told that no one had much money for gifts.

Both she and Dad would go out there at night, after they thought I was asleep. The anticipation was driving me crazy; then, finally and blessedly, Christmas came.

I rushed into the living room, and beside the tree there stood an English bicycle with its skinny little tires and all, having been practically put together from scratch by my parents with an abundance of tender loving care. My dad had operated a bicycle shop as a lad, and he was an expert. With nine more speeds, this bike would compete with anything made today.

The trouble was, I couldn't understand the wonder or worth of this bike as a small boy back then. All my friends rode what you might call in future years a "one-speed clunker," and I knew what kind of harassing I was going to take when I rolled up on this thing. A few days later, one friend's dad said something like "I say, old chap, some bloke's been whittlin' on your tires, eh wot?" That was the nicest thing anyone said.

I put on a happy face that Christmas morning, but I was right about the teasing: It was unmerciful. The old bright blue English bike, made brand new by my mom's and dad's loving hands, was years ahead of its time in small-town America.

I have only two other memories of that bike. One is pushing off a pecan tree in the back yard hundreds of times, trying to learn to ride it, and then finally one day succeeding. I remember my mother's face, filled with pride in the kitchen window, and how she ran outside to congratulate me.

The second memory is that my dad sensed why I rode it less and less, and one day he brought home a clunker frame, two rims and some tires, tubes and handlebars, sprockets and pedals. He asked me if I would like to build a good old American bike with fat tires with him, out of these parts. The smile on my face was no doubt what he had originally expected to see on that Christmas morning.

But the bike we built together was an even greater gift, for he gave of his pride and his patience, as well as his knowledge and love.

The Cat Come Back

I only knew one of my grandfathers, but he was more than enough for two. Nearly everyone can remember some old person who lighted up his life by being kind and good to him as a child; my grandfather, Dave Dill, was mine. He lived in Donaldsonville, a little town between New Orleans and Baton Rouge, but on the other side of the Mississippi River. By trade, he was a coppersmith, and he worked in a sugar mill during the grinding season and out on the plantations the rest of the year. He and his wife Bernadette had eight children, the second of whom was my mother.

My family would visit our grandparents often. It was 100 miles of bad roads to get there, and in those early 40s it took three hours, culminating in an always-delightful ferry-boat ride across the Mississippi. I loved that ferry, which was named the *George Prince*.

We were as cool as four cucumbers standing on the deck on a muggy Louisiana Friday night, watching Grandpa's little town draw closer and closer as the big boat chugged across the river with its cargo of from 20 to 30 automobiles. Years later, I was to summon enough courage to "pop the question" to Carolyn on a ferry boat, so ferries have always held a special meaning of power to me—somewhat like the way Popeye gained strength from his spinach.

I knew that as soon as we had crossed the river, we would ride off the ferry and be at Grandpa and Grandma's house in just four blocks. And that my grandparents, uncles, aunts and cousins would all come running out to greet us and embrace us with wonderful, proud hugs all around. Then we'd all go inside and there'd be a cup of delicious hot tea and some fresh-baked cookies on the stove, and never in my life since those early days have I felt as welcome as I did arriving at Grandpa and Grandma's house.

There were 16 of us grandchildren, and Grandpa loved us all. Seven of us were each at least five years older than the other nine, and of the "older cousins," I was the only boy. Grandpa always seemed to sense when I had had it with playing hopscotch and "ladies" and "dolls" and jacks, and he would rescue me and show me how to whittle and to plant seeds in his garden, or take me on a nice walk to the bakery to get some hot French bread.

But there were advantages to being the only boy. For one, I became proficient at the game of jacks. Many years later, I came home from work one day and found my daughters on the kitchen floor, engrossed in the game. "Wanta play, Dad (heh heh)?" asked Gayle. She and Meghan had planned to take me to the cleaners. But they didn't know about all the hours I had spent with my cousins on Grandma's floor, and I sat right down in my coat and tie and surprised them big-time.

In a larger sense, I really loved and admired my cousins, who took the place of the sisters I never had. This later translated all through my 38-year teaching career into a profound respect for my many hundreds of students of the fairer sex.

Grandpa taught us to play bouré (BOO' ray), a Cajun card game he dearly loved to play. When his eyes began to fail him and he said he couldn't play anymore because he was "gettin' too old to see the the spots on the cards," Aunt

Margie bought him a deck with huge numbers and large "spots" (spades, hearts, diamonds and clubs) so he could go on playing with his children and grandchildren.

We played for matchsticks and I learned how perilous that game was. You could lose all your matchsticks (go down in flames, so to speak) in no time playing bouré. This later saved me a fortune in college, when I saw guys losing all kinds of money gambling at bouré and I knew enough to stay away; in this way I suppose you could say that Grandpa contributed financially to my college education.

Ah, but what I remember best about Dave Dill was the way he would gather three or four of us up onto his knee and sing folk songs to us. The one we all remember to this day is "The Cat Come Back"—a funny little tune about a poor guy with a cat that he couldn't get rid of. Even after a nuclear war, as one verse told it, "the whole world had vanished without a chance to pray…but the cat come back, the very next day."

Years went flying by. Grandpa and Grandma died, and we cousins all grew up. I married and became a father, and learned to play the guitar. One night I thought I would play and sing "The Cat Come Back" for my daughter Gayle, but I couldn't remember much more than the title line. I was disappointed that I couldn't share a little of my Grandpa with her.

A year later, to my amazement, I saw and heard Randy Boone singing Grandpa's song on "The Virginian" on TV. I wrote and asked him if he had a copy of the words, and he actually sat down and wrote out seven verses longhand and mailed them to me. So *the cat had come back* once again, after all those years.

I remember being impressed by Grandpa's never-ending spiritual study. There was never a night when he didn't "read his books" — the Bible and his Christian Science literature. Even after he could no longer "see the spots on the pages," one of my aunts would always be there to read the Scripture to him.

Grandpa loved children more than anyone I've ever known. In part, I'm sure he got that love from Jesus himself, who got angry when his disciples tried to shoo away the children (Mk 10:13-16); raised a 12-year-old girl back to life (Luke 8:41-56); cured an epileptic boy (Luke 9:37-42); and told us of the prodigal son in Luke 15:11-32.

There was a day when three of my cousins — Mary, Janet and Giselda — and I went for a long walk and ended up on the river levee. We walked along it, then got onto a limb of a tree that had fallen down near the water. Dangling our toes in the Mississippi like four little Huck Finns, we were impervious of danger, but it turned out half the town was searching for us. A policeman discovered us and proudly brought us back to Grandpa's.

I remember some discussion among the grownups about how we should be punished. Grandpa put a stop to that. He talked about how we had been lost and could have drowned, and now we were found and everyone should be rejoicing. So that's what they all did, thank goodness. We were the prodigal cousins.

I am trying to be more like Grandpa now with my own grandchildren. It's much easier than it was when my own kids were small. Back then there were many more pressures and tensions and I was sometimes grumpy and moody, but like the cat in the song, the kids kept coming back for love and affection anyway. I, meanwhile, have mellowed in time for the new generation.

Here's a beloved photo of me with my Grandpa. He looks like he's about to give up on reading his newspaper, and sing me a certain song.

Eustace Could Pack It In
(For a Fee, Never for Free)

These days, school kids have it made when it comes to lunches. They can, as my children used to put it in the 60s and 70s, either "take" or "buy." This means they can brown bag it with a nice lunch from home, or else purchase their noon meal from an unbelievably delectable selection at school—pizza, fried chicken, hamburgers, you name it. And now my grandchildren in the 90s and 00s are just as well off.

But back in my grammar school in the 1940s, the nation was at war, and the lunches were provided free. No one brought lunch from home, nor could you buy from a delicious selection at school. And even if it had been allowed way back then, (a) what mother could worry about packing lunches for her kids when she was simultaneously fixing breakfast and praying for brothers and brothers-in-law and cousins in the military, some of whom were targets of Hitler's Nazis every day in Europe? And (b) what hard-working dad would send his hard-earned wartime coins to buy food when the successors of Louisiana Governor Huey P. Long were supplying the hot meals for free?

Those forced-down, free lunches of the forties really made us appreciate a good home-cooked meal. You will have to look hard to find an American who was a child during World War II who will ever fail to clean his or her plate. In those trying times, if you had said "Ugh" or "Yuk" about the supper, your next meal would've been breakfast the next morning if you were lucky.

There was one reason why those school lunches developed in all of us the marvelous habit of eating whatever was set in front of us. At my school, there was this terrible, unfair, rigidly-enforced rule that was set in concrete: You had to clean your plate (or rather your tray) else you weren't allowed to exit onto the playground for the lunch hour of fun. And if you missed the playground at lunchtime, a day of your life went right down the tube. For there were softball, football, kickball, basketball, volleyball, and root-the-peg games to be played, kites to be flown, yoyos and tops to be spun, fights to be watched, baseball cards to be traded, jokes to be told and heard and laughed at, songs to be whistled, bubble-gum to be chewed and its bubbles blown, sticks to be whittled, kumquats to be sucked, marbles to be shot, frogs to be caught, and girls (except for Ruth Ann) to be chased. Someone tried to chase Ruth Ann one day and she turned 180 degrees on a dime and flattened him with one punch.

So the whole world revolved not around the Sun as Copernicus had first discovered, but around that fantastic playground at lunchtime. It was where and when everything happened that was fun.

And yet, in spite of the critical importance of the lunch hour's recreation to the development, well-being, and pursuit of happiness of us kids, there was always that hated rule to worry about. If you didn't emulate Jack Sprat and his missus and lick your platter clean, you were forced to remain for an hour in that hot, smelly lunchroom which reeked of about 350 overripe, sweaty (no air-conditioning then) kiddies and teachers and their state-supported food. In the really hot months of May and September, I was never sure what was more odoriferous—us or the lunches. This was especially true on Mondays and Fridays when they dished out the red beans and rice.

They started and ended every week with those beans; it was like every week was a red beans and rice sandwich. They fed them to us that way for eight loooooooooonnng years, K through 7, which at 39 weeks of school per year totals out to 624 platefuls (platesful?) of red beans. If only the scientists had thought of a way to bottle all the gas that resulted from all those beans, the USA would have had sufficient energy to power the entire planet well into the year 3,000.

When my own kids were in school, I asked them what happened if they couldn't finish their lunch. "No problem, Dad, you just throw it away." Back in the 40s, however, it was a HUGE problem. There was no way you could get out of that lunchroom with any more than a fork, knife and spoon on your tray. The teacher on duty would patrol the lunchroom tomb of doom, guarding its massive doors with eyes like a cat. I got caught once trying to escape, and as punishment had to write 500 lines that said:

I will never ever again attempt to sneak out of the lunchroom without eating every last bite of my delicious custard.

I will also never ever again forget the smell of that awful custard, which always seemed like it was left over from a few weeks before. I decided I would rather write the lines and get a stiff hand than to eat the custard and become stiff all over from becoming a rigor mortal. I'd also rather it be Custard's Last Stand than mine.

Like any prisoner-of-war camp, there were many brave and memorable attempts to escape the lunchroom without cleaning your plate. So that he wouldn't miss an important marbles game one day, a kid named Cozmo dumped his beans under the table when the guard wasn't looking. One of the prissy, snooty girls in our class ratted him out (she spilled the beans about his spilling the beans, so to speak), and he was snatched up by the principal, right out of the marbles ring, and brought back to the scene of his crime. Poor Cozmo was made to kneel on all fours under the table and view the remains of his dastardly deed.

"CLOSER!! CLOSER!!!!" remonstrated the principal, until Cozmo's nose was practically touching the beans. At that moment, the principal grabbed Cozmo's hair and proceeded to mop the floor with his face.

The next day, a typed notice was tacked to the entrance of the lunchroom:

> Never dump your food beneath
> the table. Remember the poor
> starving children around the
> world. You may also wish to
> remember Cozmo.

The first time we saw that notice, it put the fear of God into us. Smedley remarked, "Geez, look at that. 'You may also wish to remember Cozmo.' How could anyone forget the human mop?"

"Yeah," replied J.E. "It reminds me of our preacher last Sunday, when he said, 'You may wish to remember Emma Lou Krutzburger in your prayers. Emma Lou departed this life to go and be with the Lord this past week.'"

"I thought old Cozmo was going to depart this life and go be with the Lord yesterday," I said. "He was having trouble breathing with all those beans up his nose."

We then agreed not to put so much as an old piece of gum under the table thenceforth, when Ancil opined that they could and would find the guilty party by the teeth marks. (This may have been the idea that sparked the creation of forensic science, incidentally.)

We spent that entire lunch hour trying to figure out a way to get the red beans and custard to the poor starving children, wherever they were.

That same year, the second great attempt to escape the lunchroom occurred in late spring. One of the school clowns, named Willie Q, announced with a chuckle, "Well, I've enjoyed about as many of these beans as I can stand for one day," and he threw them right out the open window when the guard wasn't looking! A Spanish boy named Felipe who was attending the school that year, and having a hard time with English, broke up and kept repeating through peals of laughter, "Los frijoles volaron por la ventana!"

His laughter was contagious, and soon everybody at the table was saying his little sentence en español and laughing up a storm, though nobody had the slightest idea what it meant. The first thing you know, the entire lunchroom was saying in cadence, louder and louder, "LOS FRIJOLES VOLARON POR LA VENTANA!"

Now my Dad, having spent eight years in Central America (where he met my Mom), spoke excellent Spanish, and I asked him that night what Felipe's sentence meant. His reply was "The beans flew out the window. I wonder why he said that?"

Meanwhile, back in the lunchroom, unbeknownst to Willie Q was that his lunch had not landed on the ground. He was headed out the lunchroom door just as Mr.

Wetterbelly—all 250 lb and 6'4" of him—was headed in, with a goodly portion of Willie Q's red beans and custard all over his head and his suit. His neck was a bristling crimson, half from anger and half from the beans.

Wetterbelly quickly elicited a confession, snatched up a spatula from the kitchen, grabbed Willie Q by the scruff of the neck and the seat of his pants, and carried him to the "ventana." He bent poor Willie Q double with his upper half out the window while whacking away at his lower half with the spatula. The next day, there was a second message on the door:

```
Never throw your food out the
window. Remember the poor
starving children around the
world. You may also wish to
remember Willie Q.
```

The third heroic attempt to escape the lunchroom with an empty but healthy stomach occurred the next year. The school braggart, Figbert, made a startling announcement at the lunch table: "I bet any sucker in dis lunchroom a dime I kin walk rat outta here wid my red beans 'n' custard on me an not *in* me. But I'm only doin' it if'n at least twenty o' y'all bet agin me."

Word of Figbert's challenge spread around the lunchroom like wildfire, and soon 46 of us had put up a dime and $4.60 was on the line, a veritable fortune in those days.

I thought of the awful licking poor Figbert was going to catch from the principal, and for a moment I felt sympathy for him, but hey, he was asking for it. Not only that, but if he succeeded, there went my popcorn at next Saturday's cowboy shoot-em-up double features. (We would see two shows at the Deluxe and then walk to the Arcade for two more. Except no one called the theaters by their names; it was "the new show" and "the old show," and that's how you can know for sure that someone grew up in Slidell in the 30s, 40s, or 50s: ask them the real names and the respective nicknames of the movie theaters.)

I wondered how Figbert was going to get his lunch out of there. All he was wearing was a T-shirt and blue jeans, but that proved enough as he began coolly and surreptitiously spooning his beans and custard into his pants pockets.

Omigosh, I thought, *he is probably going to make it.* And as the last bean disappeared from Figbert's tray, he started for the door. As he neared it, he turned and grinned and threw us a very good pun: "Heh, heh, thank y'all for the *pocket* change!"

But that day there was an extra teacher in the hall, and she noticed something unusual. "Just a moment, Figbert. Why are you walking so strangely?" The guards were always looking for suspicious mannerisms at the lunchroom exit, not unlike at airport check-ins nowadays. And Figbert did resemble the cat that swallowed the canary instead of the red beans.

"I SAID, WHY ARE YOU WALKING STRANGELY, FIGBERT?"

"Errr, well, I-er, that is, ahhhh, ummmm, and-er, I guess I dunno."

"Hands up against the wall, Figbert." The principal was summoned, and a patting down of Figbert quickly revealed four pocketsful of red beans and custard.

"OK, Figbert, the masquerade is over—Take 'em off," said the principal.

"Take my pants off? Right HERE, in front of everybody?"

"You heard me, Figbert. DROP 'EM!"

Turning as red as the crimson beans within them, Figbert took off his (now) red jeans and handed them over to the principal. He in turn passed them to that day's guard, saying, "All right, Miss Hogshead, lift 'em up and shake 'em down."

After she had done so, Figbert put his pants back on, was made to clean up his mess, and was taken to the principal's office for a paddling which had a sort of squishy sound instead of the crisp "whap-whap-whap" of ordinary whippings.

The Figbert incident, incidentally, was the coining of the word "shakedown," which was thereafter used to describe any up-against-the-wall search at the school. The word spread out from there to become part of the police vernacular of the nation and the world.

Figbert got another licking from his parents that night when his mother discovered a few beans in his jeans. He learned the meaning of double jeopardy at a young age. And of course, he was immortalized on the door the next day at lunchtime:

 Never put your food in your pocket. Remember the poor starving children around the world. You may also wish to remember Figbert.

Only twice in my eight years of grade school was there a fluke of sufficient magnitude to allow us to accidentally escape the lunchroom. The first one occurred in third grade, when the guard on duty became ill early in the lunch hour (she had forgotten to pack her lunch and had eaten in the lunchroom). When she left her post, there was a mass exodus. My brave pal Ancil led us out of there like Moses going through the Red Beans Sea to the Promised Land of the playground.

The other occasion was four years later. A smart-mouth kid named J. Dudley Digby had transferred to our school, and he had been giving just about everyone a lot of hassle. One day, he contracted the runs and had to be excused four or five times during morning classes. At lunch, he got the call again, and had to dash to the restroom.

When he returned, his red beans and custard had multiplied thirty-fold, with his tray piled over a foot high with other people's lunches. I confess that I wasn't there to record his reaction first-hand for you; I had made a contribution to his tray. I heard later, though, that his response was @#$%*&?$#@!!!!!

The next day, a funny graffiti which infuriated the principal was neatly tacked beneath his Three Commandments:

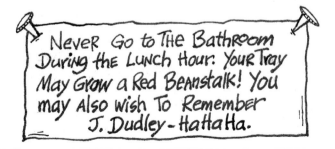

As you may surmise, windfalls like J. Dudley's Red Beans Harvest were extremely rare. Some kids went through all eight years without getting a chance to dump on someone like that (we coined that expression, too). No, there was only one way in which you could always count on escaping the lunchroom if you couldn't get your vittles down. That way was a boy with an amazing iron stomach and a flair for business, by the name of Eustace Amos Thomas. We called him by his initials, EAT, because that was what he was put on this earth for—to eat other people's lunches.

A skinny kid from the bayous, Eat had the most enormous appetite the world has ever known. He could eat for both quantity and (in the case of the lunchroom) lack of quality. To us, he was God's Gracious and Generous Gift to Gluttonous Gastrology. He was the personification of three of my comic book heroes: Jughead, Wimpy and Dagwood. But in truth, Eat could've outgorged all three of those paper heros rolled into one. After all, each of those characters specialized in delicious two-dimensional sandwiches of their own making and choosing, while our man had to eat red beans and custard in real life, Mondays in and Fridays out.

I am sure that the rumor was true—that all Eat had to eat at home was alligator meat—because he always seemed to love and appreciate whatever they set before us, be it the exception (comestible), or the rule (not).

But let me tell you, Eat wasn't dumb. He knew how badly we all wanted out of that lunchroom every day. And so there was a fee. Eat got filthy rich eating other people's lunches. He earned a veritable ton of spending money with that voracious appetite of his. And the more disgusting the dish, the higher was his price to gobble it up for you. The minimum fee for a serving of red beans and rice was 15¢ for the first one he ate on a given day, 20¢ for the second, and a quarter thereafter. Spinach was 20¢, and that awful custard was always a quarter.

On some days, Eat would stagger out of the lunchroom a whole *dollar* richer. To give you an idea how much buying power a dollar had in those days in the forties, a movie was 9¢, a big candy bar or a coke or a bag of popcorn was a nickel, and the allowance of the richest kid in town was 30¢. (Mine was a dime.) Since a movie today costs eight bucks, which is 89 times nine cents, Eat's take in today's dollars was 89 times a dollar, or $89. In nine months of school per year times five days a week, he was raking in $17,355 in today's dollars just eating red beans and custard. Amazing. Here is a sketch of Eat as I remember him, devouring both our lunches and our money:

Eat amassed a fortune in seven years. When we went to high school, though, he was in for a rude awakening. We no longer had to clean our plates in order to be excused from the new lunchroom, and so Eat was out of a job. As soon as he turned 16, he dropped out of school and I never saw him again. It was rumored that he bought his own bayou together with a fleet of pirogues and a worm ranch and fished away the rest of a long life off the spoils of spoiled food and spoiled kids.

Eustace Amos Thomas, bless his heart—or rather his stomach—was as close as this world has ever come to a bottomless pit. I am thankful to this day that we had him there to Eat for us when we needed him.

EPILOGUE:

For many years after grade school, I wouldn't go near a red bean. But one night Carolyn and I were invited over to Edna and Gerry Deckbar's home for dinner. Edna, one of the world's great cooks, served up some red beans and rice and ham hocks. To my amazement, they were delicious. On the way home that night, I forgave Huey P. Long and my home town's free-lunch program in my heart.

Bubby and Mrs. Sippi

About a year before I retired, I was on my way home one evening using public transportation. I got off the MARTA train and boarded the 91 bus that would take me to my neighborhood. There were perhaps a dozen people on the bus, waiting for the driver who was on a short break.

I was sitting in the first row of forward-facing seats, on the left side of the aisle. In front of me were two longer bench seats, the occupants of which faced the center line of the bus, i.e., faced one another. There was a man on the right-hand bench, and a couple seated on the left. The rest of the occupants were behind me.

Suddenly, the man up ahead of me on the right began to shake all over, and make loud, groaning sounds. His eyes rolled up in their sockets, and his head was banging violently against the support pole.

The couple at the left hurried off the bus, as I went quickly to the man's assistance. All the rest of the occupants cleared out also, except for a woman named Sally, who frantically asked me, "What's wrong with him? What can we do?" I knew exactly what to tell her. I had been well-trained, as a boy.

"He is having an epileptic seizure," I said. "We have to get him lying down on this bench, making sure he's not choking, then hold him in place and comfort him until it passes, in several minutes at most."

Which we did. After a time, we then helped the man off the bus, and the driver, who had just returned, assisted him in calling his family. The woman asked, "How did you know what to do? Are you a doctor?"

"No," I replied. "But I used to help Bubby." I explained further, drawing on a recollection that went back nearly 50 years to an incident that occurred in the sixth grade. It involved a person, and a colossal failure on my part to help him. On that day I let Bubby down, and I've never forgotten it....

One day our teacher Miss Craddock told four of us boys to stay after school, that she wanted to talk with us. I wish she had informed us at the *end* of the day; we nervously wondered all day long what we had done wrong, when in fact (for once) we hadn't done anything. She gathered five chairs in a circle and we sat down, and then she spoke.

"Boys, there is a new student joining our class tomorrow. His name is Bubby. I am going to need help with him and that is why you are here. Do you boys know what epilepsy is?" We didn't, so she continued: "Bubby is an epileptic. He is likely to have an attack, or seizure, at any time. He will lose consciousness, and may fall to the floor. His muscles will contract in spasms, and these convulsions will usually last about three minutes. Bubby has the most severe form, called grand mal. Do you have any questions so far?"

"Errr, is it catchin'?" asked one of us, fearfully.

"No. Epilepsy is not contagious in the least. Now, I have selected you four young men because you're either smart or strong or both. I will seat one of you on Bubby's left, one on his right, one in front, and one in back of his desk.

"The moment any of you sees that Bubby is entering a seizure, just say 'Help.' I then expect the four of you to drop everything and work together to get him safely onto the floor, then hold him securely until the attack passes.

There will then be a complete relaxation, and things will return to normal. Any more questions?"

There were none, and Miss Craddock went into a few more details such as prevention of choking, and then we were dismissed.

The next day, we all met Bubby. He was a big boy, very strong yet extremely gentle. He was always smiling, and when he wasn't in the classroom, humming and singing.

I didn't get any class work done that morning. I was constantly glancing at Bubby to see if he was OK; the four of us were taking our new responsibility very seriously.

We didn't have to wait very long, as the first attack came that very afternoon. It was frightening, to be sure, but after a fortnight passed and Bubby had had two more seizures, we were handling it well. But Bubby was experiencing other problems.

Nearly every child who differs from the norm in some way automatically has a second problem—he or she gets picked on. Bubby was no exception; his classmates, and especially the bullies, were always putting him down and leaving him out of games.

One day a lot of kids were standing around at recess, and Bubby walked up. The talk was about songs, and Bubby asked, "Say, did anyone hear 'Mr. and Mrs. Sippi'?"

I listened to the radio some, and just the day before, I had heard the new song to which Bubby was referring. It was about the Mississippi River making an orphan feel at home. (The song, sung by Patti Page, was actually titled "Mister and Mississippi.") I had liked it, but before I could say so, some of the bullies started in on poor Bubby:

"WHA-A-A-A-AT? What kind of a stupid name is that? There's no song like that."

"But I heard it on my radio last night," protested Bubby.

"No you didn't," said another of the class bullies, "because there's *no such song*." And he shoved Bubby to the ground.

"There really is a song like that , no matter what you do to me," Bubby replied bravely.

The bullies, not used to back-talk, then forced Bubby to spell "Mississippi" the funny way—you know, "M–I–Crooked Letter, Crooked Letter–I–Crooked Letter, Crooked Letter–I–Humpback, Humpback–I." He couldn't say it right, and after 15 minutes of torture and taunts, the bell blessedly rang.

Bubby had looked at me for help, because he always felt close to the four of us who helped him through his seizures, and I was the only one around. But I was just like Peter in the courtyard on Good Friday: I didn't know the man, or in this case the song, when it really counted.

I could have spared Bubby that awful experience by simply speaking up and admitting what I knew to be the truth. But I had allowed the peer pressure and fear of the bullies to block me out, and I trampled on the downtrodden just as surely as if I had been one of those guys giving him the spelling lesson.

Bubby left school after that one year with us. I grew into adulthood, and I thought of him from time to time. I heard that certain drugs were now helping epileptics to control and even to prevent attacks such as those Bubby had suffered so often. I hoped that he had lived to experience the miraculous relief that I was hearing about. It turned out that he had. I saw him one more time, many years later.

I was riding to see my parents on a Greyhound bus, and it was at the end of the day. The bus stopped in the middle of nowhere, and a big man from somewhere in the back of the bus passed my seat, humming as he went, and got off.

He was wearing blue-collar work clothes, carrying a lunch pail and a newspaper, and he was clearly a happy fellow with a good, honest job.

"I *know* that guy," I thought to myself. And as the bus roared off, the man's face flashed past my window. As you have guessed, it was Bubby. He was singing as he walked, but I couldn't tell what.

Probably "Mr. and Mrs. Sippi." There really was a song like that, you know.

I Never Lost My Marbles

When I finished grade school I owned literally thousands of marbles. They filled eight U.S. Army ammunition containers to the brim, and each of those metal boxes was, from memory, about 4 inches wide, 15 inches long, and a foot high; thus, each one held a lot of marbles. Except for the little bag I had started with in third grade, every marble had been either won or traded for, and each of them had its own story to tell.

Pack-rat that I am, I hated to part with the marbles when I left home. I compromised by filling a little leather bag with as many of my favorites as it would hold, and I kept those. The rest I gave to some little neighborhood kids, and as the game of marbles was still king in grade school, it was the windfall of their lives. They could be the worst players in Slidell history and still shoot marbles for years and never lose them all.

One of the marbles in the sack, which I still have, is an orange agate with a slight chip on its surface. It was quite a famous marble in its day. It was my "shooter," and it brings back memories even after a half-century of time.

If you asked me what I was most skilled at in this life, I would answer that shooting marbles would be way up there near the top. It was one of only three things I did righthanded as a boy. The others were, and still are, writing and eating, and that needs a paragraph of explanation.

For some reason—maybe it was all the assembly lines in nearby shipbuilding plants in the early 40s, necessitated by World War II—many parents were trying to get their left-handed toddlers to switch, and mine were no exception.

My dad brought home this box of little plastic airplanes, 100 of them and each one unique. As I started first grade, Dad said that for each day I wrote and ate right-handed, I could have one of the planes. He figured that after three months, if I wrote and ate right-handed, I would be doing everything else right-handed. But it didn't work; although I earned all the airplanes, to this day I do everything else left-handed. For the life of me I don't know why marble-shooting was the exception, but it was. When my brother came along five years later, Dad didn't even try to change him; he does everything left-handed.

The bizarre thing about my right-handed marble-playing was that there were only four better players in the school, and all of them—Richard, Jackson, Ronnie and Junior—were left-handed. I got so frustrated trying to beat those guys that I once tried to switch; but in spite of the fact that I was a true lefty, I wasn't as good from the port side and I eventually had to settle for fifth-best. (For a while there I was the only switch-hitting, or rather switch-shooting, marbles player in my school.)

There was a thrill to playing marbles that I've rarely felt elsewhere. Marbles was a rare combination of skill and gambling in which there was (a) almost a complete absence of luck; (b) physical skill and mental determination required, on which success utterly depended; and (c) there were the marbles themselves, multi-colored and shiny, to be either won and cherished, or lost and pined for. With cards, it was the luck of the draw with no physical skill needed, and can you imagine playing cards and winning some of the cards?

And so we played marbles. By the light of the Sun and, many nights, by the light of the Moon as well. Every kid practiced in his neighborhood, honing and polishing his skills in preparation for the bigger wars at school, played at recess, lunchtime, and after school.

THE RULES OF THE GAME

To play, a ring was drawn with someone's pocket knife on the ground, about four feet in diameter. Everyone playing put a marble in the center of the ring, and if there were four or more, they were stacked into little piles with three of them forming a tight triangle on the bottom and the fourth resting on top. Sometimes the "ante" was raised to two or more, and in a given game there might be four or five piles in there.

Next we would "lag up," which meant that you tossed your shooter toward the opposite side of the ring to determine the order of play, the closest to the circle shooting first. It was of crucial importance to be a good lagger if you were a world-class player like I (humbly) was, because if you shot last in a big game against those lefties, you would soon be like the poor fellow who invested half his money in paper towels and the other half in revolving doors, who was wiped out before he could turn around.

When it became your turn, you would shoot by propelling your shooter marble from any point just outside the circle, aiming it at the marbles within the ring. Any that you knocked out of the ring were yours to keep, and your turn ended when you "missed," or failed to knock anything out.

Now it was of prime importance to own a good "sticker," which was a shooter with the mysterious quality of staying put, or "sticking," whenever it zapped a marble and sent it rolling on its way out of the ring. This is known in dynamics, I now realize, as transferring all of its momentum into the other marble. A good sticker was invaluable, for it allowed the player to successively take aim at the remaining marbles at close range in the center of the ring. In short, one could really mop up with a good sticker.

JUNIOR'S AMAZING INVENTION

One of the four lefties who could beat me at marbles was a boy named Junior, aka the Sticker King. Junior was a frail kid with a big smile, kind to everyone except those of us who were his marbles opponents. He had a job on the weekends working at Mr. Pete's service station, fixing cars and pumping gas. Years later, I gassed up at Mr. Pete's, and Junior was still working there. We reminisced about some of the great marbles players and games of the past. He was the best, and this was due in no small measure to a major innovation he made in the game.

Junior was famous for his invention of the "steelie," as we came to call it (although we should've named it a "junior" in his honor). It was a formidable weapon in the right hands, or rather the right "hand," or in Junior's case, the *left* hand.

One Saturday in the course of his work, Junior came across some little ball bearings. In the same accidental way that great discoveries such as penicillin were made, Junior looked in his hand and as the steel balls went clackety, a light in his head went clickety. As soon as he clocked out, he ran home to his marbles ring and discovered that when the little steel ball bearing was used as a shooter, two wonderful things simultaneously occurred: (1) any marble hit by it was a goner, and (2) the "steelie" stuck in the ring like glue.

Now Junior was small, but he became a giant with his invention. However, he was forced to develop his skill with little bitty steelies, only 1/4 or 3/8 inch in diameter. This was because anything larger was likely to destroy the marbles it struck. Junior had a ball with his little steelies, but his invention didn't have much of a bearing on the rest of us, because no one but Junior ever developed sufficient ability with those small steels to make a living at it— everyone else's fingers were too big.

WINNERS, PLOOPERS AND THE SQUIRTER

Quite a few of my schoolmates never learned how to properly grip a marble so as to shoot for both power and accuracy. This always seemed odd to me, since there were really only three ways of holding a shooter: the right way, the wrong way, and J.E. Crow's way.

Winning Stance   Losing Stance   J.E.'s Stance

If one was a winner at marbles, and there were no exceptions, he (more about "she" later) held his shooter as shown on the left in the sketch above. The secret of the power was that the thumb was gripped against the palm with the middle finger, which allowed it 32 extra degrees of travel, according to my protractor. After aiming, the index finger straightened as the thumb exploded outward, propelling the shooter toward its target at high speed.

Now and then a truly outstanding shot would crash into a pile of four marbles and knock two or three of them out of the ring. There was simply no greater feeling than that. You would strut around, picking up and pocketing your winnings and then returning to the ring for possible further glory. The psyche effect of all this was very important—kind of like the pro football players doing their silly little dances in the end zone—and no one was better at it than a player named Jackson Beauregard (who must've had a Rebel ancestor who played marbles during breaks in the Civil War).

Jackson was to marble-shooting what Lee Marvin was to gunslinging in his Oscar-winning role in the movie *Cat Ballou*. Jackson always dressed the part, with fancy patches on the knees of his jeans, and a jingling black leather sack dangling from his belt with the words "USED TO BE YOUR MARBLES" sewn on in brightly colored capital letters.

And there was the bandanna. Jackson had a flaming red bandanna, which he carefully folded prior to each round of games, while glaring into the eyes of his opponents. They knew what that bandanna was for. He placed it on the ground beneath his left hand before each shot so as not to dirty his knuckles. When it came his turn to shoot, Jackson would spin his shooter onto the ground and then calmly position the bandanna *before the shooter had stopped spinning*. This drove such fear into the hearts of the weaker players that they lost their marbles before they lost their marbles, so to speak. Jackson understood that "silent trash-talking" made his opponents think and then become afraid, as compared to the loud type of hype which only inspires anger and often promotes even better play.

There was a legitimate ripoff known as "razzoo" in the game of marbles as we played it. When the bell rang calling us back to classes, it was permissible to grab any marbles still in the ring with a shout of "RAZZOO!" and keep them. And there was one little runt named Elmer who had nine sisters and no brothers who was a lousy shot at marbles, but who was like a human vacuum cleaner at razzoo. When but a minute or two remained until the bell rang, he would quickly scout all the games to see which ring contained the most marbles, then at the bell he'd pounce into the ring like a cat.

Elmer's hands were like greased lightning as they swished over the ring, scooping up all the marbles before anyone else even had time to bend over. I asked him once how he came to be so good at razzoo, and he put me off by saying it was the only way he could get any of his lost marbles back. I pressed him, and he finally told me after I swore never to reveal his secret: "I been playin' jacks with all my sisters since I was old enough to bounce the rubber ball." This I understood perfectly, because I, too, had become proficient at jacks by playing the game with all my girl cousins. I, however, didn't parlay my jacks ability into razzooing like Elmer did. The great players wouldn't lower ourselves to razzoo; we divided the marbles left in the ring whenever the bell rang, like civilized people.

Elmer pushed his luck too far one day. He razzooed a game in which Jackson, Ronnie and Richard were playing. Any one of those guys could've swept up the ring using Elmer as a broom, and here he was razzooing all three of them. I can still picture him standing poised near that game, watching his watch. The bell rang, and Elmer yelled, "RAZZOOEY! WAHOOEY!" and he jumped into the ring and swept up the marbles. He sprang up with them, ready to head for the school building. But there were the three enforcers—the biggest and strongest guys in the school— each spanning 120 degrees of the circle, glaring inward at him.

In a flash Elmer's blue jeans were separated from him and the marbles were shaken out of them and returned to their rightful owners. Then, still in his drawers, Elmer was carried quickly to the artesian well and baptised in it with full immersion. Finally, his jeans were tossed up in a tree while everyone else returned to the classroom.

Now our teacher that year was Mrs. Ratliff. She was the toughest teacher I ever had, and one of the very best as well. She maintained a discipline of iron by means of a paddle we called "The Termite." It came about that nickname because there were little holes drilled through the wood in strategic spots, to increase the velocity on the downstroke. That paddle had worn out thousands of rebellious pupils' rear ends. Once you had been paddled by The Termite, you could be certain that all the evil in you had been exterminated.

"Where is Elmer?" asked Mrs. Ratliff, annoyed that a seat would dare to be empty following recess.

"He's out climbin' a tree, Mrs. Ratliff," answered Ronnie. Whereupon she walked to the window, peered out, and sure enough, there was Elmer retrieving his pants, up in the tree.

Mrs. Ratliff, Termite in hand, stalked angrily out of the classroom and headed for the playground. The entire class was lined up at the window to observe the carnage. Elmer had pulled on his wet pants in the fork of the huge oak, but he could've saved himself the trouble, because no sooner had Mrs. Ratliff dragged him to the ground than he had to drop the pants again and grab his ankles so as to be in position to receive an unfriendly visit from The Termite.

After Elmer's bad day, no one razzooed for a month. Just thinking about Mrs. Ratliff's infamous paddle was enough to send chills down your spine, all the way to your gluteus maximus.

I should also mention the *wrong* way to shoot a marble. Whenever we saw someone gripping their shooter between the index finger and the thumbnail (see the middle sketch), we knew that poor devil's marbles bag was ripe for the plucking. We called such an incompetent a "plooper," because his shooter merely rolled along lazily, sort of like ploop-ploop-ploop. A plooper never had the velocity to win at the game; nevertheless, in spite of their heavy losses and their ever-sore thumb cuticles, most ploopers never figured out their problem. And we weren't about to tell them. Except for my pal Tubby.

Tubby was one of the worst ploopers of all time. Bless his heart, he must've lost five thousand marbles (that's about five a day) over a fruitless five-year career. I tried for years to teach Tubby how to shoot, but, alas, he had terminal lazy-thumb disease and never did overcome it. In later life, Tubby became a successful banker, and I am pleased to report that he was infinitely better at managing other people's money than he had been with his own marbles.

I won so many marbles from another sucker/plooper that his father took action. He hired a hit man—or rather a hit kid—to beat me up. Lordy, that was awful. I took the licking, even getting in one good lucky punch myself, but

I'm proud to say that I refused to surrender the marbles as demanded by the shakedown artist. The plooper was twice my weight and taller, and I had won those marbles fair and square.

My buddy J.E. was an anomaly in grade school marbles. He had the "fastest thumb in the south," and yet he rarely ever won. He would actually squeeze the marble out from between his thumb and the outside of his index finger (see the third sketch). The shooter would then squirt at supersonic speed in the general direction of the target. J.E. was the marbles counterpart of baseball's Sandy Koufax in his early years as a pitcher: fast as greased lightning but wild as kudzu.

Only on rare occasions would J.E.'s shooter collide with a stack of marbles in the ring, but when it did, let me tell you that marbles were splattered all over the playground. Even if he barely clipped one, enough of a component of force was imparted to send it flying on its way out of the ring.

J.E. received countless accolades and was known far and wide in marble circles for his unorthodox style; no one else could even come near the target shooting, or rather squirting, that way. There could be a big game going on for sky-high stakes (like putting up shooters in the ring as ante, for example), and yet if J.E. was playing nearby, everyone would gather to watch him instead. The chance to see and hear the squirt-shooter connect would draw a huge crowd every time.

Unlike Koufax, though, J.E. never got control of his control. He was unable to perfect his accuracy to the level necessary to play world-class marbles.

BAD BULL STEALS THE BIG STEELS

Once each year, a certain "Colossal, Stupendous and Tremendous" circus would stop in Slidell for a few days on its annual trek across the South.

All the youngsters would hop onto their bikes and head for the site to watch the workers erect the big tents and the rides. On one such day, part of the ferris wheel collapsed, strewing broken parts all over the place. And amidst the wreckage, the school bully made and pocketed a discovery which was to wreak havoc in marbles circles for months and very nearly annihilate our beloved game from the grounds of the school.

Poking around the circus grounds where the ferris wheel had stood, "Bull" — as he was appropriately called — found a pair of humongous ball bearings. Each of them was a couple of inches in diameter. Bull stole them, and it was amazing that they got the ferris wheel back together without them, for those "big steels" were never to return to the circus.

Now Bull had always hated and avoided marbles games. He was a monster but also a klutz (the only thing he knew how to do with his hands was to make, and use, a fist), and marbles was the only game at which he could get "whupped" by scrawny yet skilled and disciplined bags of bones like Junior and me. It was also the only sport at which he couldn't destroy his opponents by the threat and/or use of force; and so it was the only sport he hated, and he did so unmercifully. But once he had those two big steels, he became the proverbial wild Bull in the china closet—except that the closet was a marbles ring.

It was awful. Bull began to enter games and shoot by "bowling" his big steel boulders at the imperiled marbles.

This technique had been tried using ordinary marbles; it had proved unsuccessful, however, because the accuracy wasn't nearly as good as that of the better players shooting normally.

The monster steels, however, were so gigantic (512 times the volume of Junior's little steelies) that accuracy was no longer a problem, and Bull started cleaning up. To give you an idea of the mass of those steel spheres, one damp day they rolled into the ring and just flat squashed their targets into the wet earth. We had no rule to cover that situation, so Bull snatched them up, growling, "Ah planted 'em, so ah'll harvest 'em."

Within a week, Big Bad Bull was making a shambles of our beloved game. He bragged that he was going to drive the game of marbles right off the playground and across town and into Lake Pontchartrain. Each day he would bowl another hundred or so marbles into oblivion. They were helpless against the onslaught, and those that didn't shatter upon impact were scooped up by Bull and flung with a curse into the canal that surrounded the playground. I hated that with a passion; I loved both the game and the marbles themselves, and I winced and gritted my teeth each time a perfectly good marble was broken or wasted.

AGATHA THE AGATE-HEAD

Now there was only one great marbles player at our school who was of the gentle sex. Truth to tell, Agatha wasn't very gentle, but we really liked and respected her— both for her ability at marbles and also for the way she took the abuse from the other girls for playing marbles with the boys. They called her "Agatha the Agate-Head," and chided and derided her endlessly about her dirty right knuckles and her filthy knees.

But as hard as it was for Agatha to put up with the girls' taunting, there was to be an incident in her life that was far more painful but which was to result in the restoration of marbles to its revered place on the school playground.

Bull despised Agatha, not only because he hated *all* girls, and not only because she could beat him to a pulp at marbles, but also because she, being a female, was living proof that it was possible for everyone in the *world* to end up playing and enjoying the one game at which he was a hopeless and hapless loser, and at which he couldn't bully his way to victory.

One day Bull decided to accelerate his destruction of the game of marbles by renting out one of the big steels for a nickel a day. I was so proud of us all—NOBODY accepted his offer. He stood there, furious and fuming, and then Agatha burned him good when she popped up and said, "Why don't you go rent 'em to the circus, where you stole 'em from in the first place?"

Sporting the reddest neck in the history of the South, Bull cursed and challenged Agatha to a high-stakes game of "shooters." This was the equivalent of a duel, in which you didn't risk your life, but (at that age) the closest thing to it: your best shooter.

Now Bull's shooter wasn't worth much, but Agatha's meant the world to her. It was beautiful—yellow with a blue streak across one side and a red one across the other—and very much admired on the playground by all us players. Agatha's pet name for this cherished marble was "Streaky."

To our horror, she accepted Bull's challenge. She thought she could win the lag and then clean up before Bull could bowl one of his big steels at her beloved shooter. But she lost the lag, and Bull wasted no time in smacking Streaky out of the ring.

There followed a despicable, heinous, disgusting act that Bull was to regret for years to come: He pounced upon Streaky, jammed it part-way into the ground, and flung those hideous, massive, steel ball bearings down upon it over and over and over again, until it was reduced to a pile of tiny yellow, blue and red chips. Agatha choked back her tears and ran to the girls' restroom.

THE END OF THE CRISIS

The next day, shortly before dismissal, a student returning to his classroom from the restroom took a mysterious sidetrip past the principal's office and slipped beneath the door a crudely printed note stating that Bull had been smoking during recess that afternoon and still had a pack of cigarettes in his pocket; he knocked on the door, then hightailed it safely back to his classroom.

The timing was superb. Just two minutes later, Bull was called to the principal's office over the intercom, and scolded, paddled severely, and made to sit in the corner wearing the famous dunce cap for an hour. And three minutes after the bell rang for school dismissal, the big steels of Bad Bull vanished from his desk and from his life and ours forever.

Bull never played another game of marbles. It was rumored that he had misplaced his big steels, but nobody seemed to know what had become of them. (For sure, if anyone did, he wasn't telling for fear of his life.) But nobody cared, either, just so long as they stayed gone, because marbles had returned to its great popularity. Pockets jingled and kids smiled and knuckles and knees got dirty as marbles once again rolled on the playground.

Each of the good players gave Agatha their second-best shooter, and the story of her sacrifice became a legend in the little town.

EPILOGUE

Many years later, while back in my hometown for a reunion, I went by the old grade school. I parked my car and strolled out on the playground. Noting that it was still there, I walked onto the bridge over the canal, over which I used to walk as I headed home each afternoon for seven years in the 40s and early 50s.

I looked out over the muddy water, and something from long, long ago flashed across my mind. I grinned as I recalled the story I have just told you. And for a moment there, I could feel those two big steel eyes, glaring angrily at me from their grave somewhere along the murky bottom of the canal.

Smedley Was the Very First Streaker

I have an old newspaper clipping from 1982 which relates (FLASH!!!) how some poor devil was sentenced to 99 years in jail for exposing himself. I remember cutting out the exposé because of the incongruity between his fate and that of the thousands of college streakers eight years before, who were for the most part merely snickered at by the police. The guy who went to prison just plain and simply streaked too late; the fad was long since past.

Yes, everybody was taking it all off in 1974, and wherever you went, you had a good chance of seeing someone suddenly dash across your path in the raw. Such a person was known as a streaker.

The nudist colonies were getting concerned there for a while, because it was beginning to look like there was nothing unique about them.

Now as it is with any craze, streaking was especially popular at the colleges and universities across the country. Even at staid old Georgia Tech, where I taught for 33 years, there was a streak-in one moonlit night involving hundreds of students, including coeds. I saw one of my students in the photo accompanying the newspaper article, and the next day after class I said to him, "I saw in the paper that you weren't working your dynamics problems last night. At the streak-in, you got a little behind in your work, didn't you? (heh, heh)." I shouldn't have done that—it was below the belt, and I never saw anyone as embarrassed as that.

If they were streaking at Georgia Tech, wherein resided the most conservative student body on Earth, then you know they were disrobing everywhere. Why, in the riotous 60s and 70s, the only protesting that Tech students ever did was when a few of them burned their yearbooks when nobody liked the way they came out.

Once during the craze I was riding home from work just after dark, and I looked up in the sky and saw not one, but two full moons. I slowed down to get a better look, and the non-celestial moon was someone's rear end in puris naturalibus hanging out the window of a fraternity house. I turned the other cheek and drove off, thinking that I had just seen the bottom half of the lewdest lunar moonie since the Wolfman.

The incomparable Ray Stevens made everybody laugh with a recording on the radio entitled "The Streak." The song was about an inveterate streaker, and these were some of its hilarious, poetic lines:

"Here he comes, there he goes....and he ain't wearin' no clothes!"

"Oh, yes, they call him the streak....he likes to give us a peek!"

"He ain't crude, he ain't lewd....he just likes to run around in the nude!"

In the song, a man and his wife Ethel kept seeing the streaker everywhere they went—in the farmer's market, at the gas station, and finally at a packed-house basketball game. And every time, Ethel, in a flash, would strip and chase after the guy with a "boogedy, boogedy" sound effect. The last time, Ethel didn't come back—she liked what she saw and was having too much fun.

At the Academy Awards Oscars show, when a streaker ran right across the stage behind presenter David Niven, he made a brilliant recovery and said that all the poor guy would ever be remembered for would be his shortcomings.

During the craze, I recall pondering what it might feel like to do a little meek streak around the back yard. But I quickly erased the thought because it was freezing out and something important might get frostbitten, and secondly Carolyn would've locked the door behind my behind and called for the men with the straightjackets. She was not a buff of the buff.

Thirdly, and this time truthfully, the last time I had been disrobed in front of anyone except my wife, I was nearly killed. IN MY OWN DOCTOR'S OFFICE!!! I was undergoing a physical, and it came time for the bottom line—the dreaded proctoscope.

Just at the moment when my gluteus maximus was cranked up to the apex, the upper half of the examining table broke loose, and I rode it down in rectilinear motion as it slid to the floor and crashed into the wall. Dazed, for a few seconds there I didn't know which end was up any more.

"Call a doctor," I mumbled weakly.

"I *am* a doctor," said my doctor.

"Then call another doctor," I replied.

Actuarily, my doctor could've killed me. It is a good thing for him that he is also my friend, because no malpractice jury in the world, imagining themselves in my strange predicament, would fail to award me a fortune. My doctor friend would've been in arrears to me forever for that kind of double-jeopardy torture.

The reason I know I didn't dream that experience, by the way, is that the hole in the sheetrock above the baseboard, where it was struck by me and the procto table, is still there in the rear wall to this very day. There should be a plaque there, marking the spot like they do in baseball parks for historic home runs:

> ON THIS SPOT IN 1976
> DAVE McGILL KEPT HIS
> BUNNY-SIDE UP THROUGHOUT
> THE MOST DEATH-DEFYING,
> PERILOUS PROCTOSCOPIC
> PEREGRINATION IN HISTORY…
> AND LIVED TO WRITE ABOUT IT.

For all proctoscopes since then, I have made sure my seat belt was fastened.

Returning to streaking, it was not known to all those who took it off in 1974 that they were fully twenty years behind the times. An old pal of mine had performed the very first streak at our high school in May of 1953. I am taking the liberty of discounting two better-known historical streaks for the following reasons:

(1) Lady Godiva is ineligible because the true streak involves a scamper and not a ride on a horse. Also, her long hair covered over whatever the saddle didn't cover under.

(2) When Archimedes discovered the principle of buoyancy, he is purported to have leapt from his bathtub and dashed stark naked through the streets, shouting deliriously, "I've found it! I've found it!" Old Arch is also ruled out as the first streaker, because the poor devil didn't even know what he was doing at the time. All he was conscious of was that a floating body displaces its own weight of water.

And so the first to freely flee in the flesh was not Lady Godiva or Archimedes. In fact, the Premier and Preeminent Streaker of Earth has up to now unselfishly remained unsung. I shall now proceed to strip bare the secrets of his identity and to reveal to you my first-hand account of how he came to win his title.

There were 40 people in my high school graduating class. About ten of us had begun kindergarten on the same day in September 1944 and then proceeded through 13 tough years of schooling together. One of those classmates was my pal E. Z. Smedley. He hated his first name, Elishaphat, and his middle name, Zerubbabel, was even worse, so he went through school as Smedley. In retrospect, we should've nicknamed him E. Z. or "Easy," but I guess no one thought of it at the time.

From day one in the first grade, Smedley and I were always getting teased unmercifully by our schoolmates because we were so skinny. The standing joke they would play on Smedley was to pretend that he was so thin that he disappeared when viewed from the side. Whenever he walked up to a group, everyone would pretend not to notice him; then, when he spoke for the first time, they would say, "Hey, I thought I just heard Smedley! Anyone seen Smedley?" There would ensue a mock search, until finally Ancil would walk around and notice Smedley head-on and say, "Oh, here he is, guys! He was invisible because he was turned sideways!"

Smedley would then invariably give his stock reply to these shenanigans: "Think ya funny, huh?"

Because we each took so much harassment over being bony, Smedley and I naturally each joined in when the other was being put down. This resulted in several awful knock-down-and-drag-out fights between the two of us, but in high school we ended up good friends.

The streaking episode occurred in the eighth grade. That year, my physical education class met during fourth period, just before lunch. In the class were most of the juniors and seniors on the football team, and six of us who were "subbies" (sub-freshmen): Ancil, J.E., Tubby, Tony, Smedley and me.

What the six of us dreaded most about school that entire year was going into a little undersized locker room to dress after P. E. class. The football players ragged us unmercifully every day.

Sometimes they threw us into the showers with all our clothes on, and occasionally they locked one or two of us in our lockers so we would miss lunch. Once, that became a "blessing before the meal," because they all got food poisoning from one of the free lunches while our stomachs were locked up safe and sound. The only trouble was that they were too sick to remember to set us free, and my mom was concerned about my suddenly altered, cramped and stoop-shouldered posture for a week until I finally straightened out.

One day they tossed our socks in the showers and hid our shoes, and we had to walk around all afternoon in wet socks. I remember that our toes got mangled in the stampedes between classes even though we tried to tiptoe around in our stocking feet. One of the monsters saw me struggling to class and yelled out for all the hall to hear: "Hey!!! Lookit McGill!!! Doin' a little ballet for us! Dance purty, now, Little David!" I hated that day.

One of the seniors noticed that Tubby, who was very rotund, wore the same brand of briefs as Smedley, and he swapped their drawers in their lockers while they were still out on the field. The rest of that day, Tubby looked sort of flushed and uncomfortable—as if not enough blood was reaching the lower extremities of his body—while Smedley kept hitching up his trousers as if something was falling down within them, which it was.

All that year, that cursed locker room was the birthplace of a form of Murphy's Law: *If anything else can be done unto us, it will be.* And it was, big time.

One beautiful day in May, we had just come into the locker room after P.E. and removed our gym shorts, when one of the monsters (the one we called Frankenstein because he was the spitting image of Boris Karloff without the iron bar sticking through his neck) shouted, "Hey, y'all!!! I know a favor what we can do for them subbies today!" (He didn't talk any better than he looked.)

"All right, then, let's hear it, man!" said another. (We called him Dracula because he hung around with Frankenstein.)

"OK, let's give the little peewees some SUNSHINE!!! They all look a little pale, don't you think?"

"Yeah!! Haw, haw!! A shot of vitamin D will do 'em good," said the Wolfman. (We had names for all of them.)

Oh, Lord, I knew right away what they were talking about. It was something I had hoped and prayed they would never think of—throwing us out of that locker room onto the football field buck naked, or as we say in the South, NEKKID—with hundreds of coeds and teachers strolling by on their way to and from lunch on a walkway adjacent to the door.

They moved menacingly toward us. I can remember a useless little conversation I had with myself inside my head, that went something like this:

"How do I get out of here?" I asked.

"Dummy, you don't want to get *out*, you want to stay *in*," I replied.

"No, I don't want to do that either," I answered. What a discombobulating moment that was. I didn't want to go, and I didn't want to stay. But reality snapped me out of it, and I quickly looked around. Cowering there with fear registering and growing on our faces, we didn't exactly look like those athletes doing underwear commercials, let me tell you.

Ancil, Tony, and Tubby stood there in their briefs, while J.E. and I were attired only in our striped and polkadotted boxers, respectively.

And then I saw Smedley. Ye gods, what a sight.

Clad only in his socks, and knowing what was coming, Smedley was frantically rooting like a mole in the bottom of his locker, trying desperately but futilely to locate his underwear.

"Hey, Smedley baby, looking for these?" sneered a voice from across the little room. Frankenstein held up Smedley's undershorts in his clenched fist, and bellowed, "FRUIT OF THE LOOMS!!! WHAT AM I BID FOR THESE FINE DRAWERS?!!" And they held a mock auction, inching ever closer to us as they bid. Poor Smedley bid his last dollar for his own underwear, but those awful, taunting creatures weren't interested in money that day.

"Shouldn't we let their little BEhinds get a little sun tan?" shouted Dracula.

"Good idea! Let's strip 'em all and pitch 'em to the wolves, man," said the Wolfman.

"Course now Smedley, there, he's already dressed for the party, ain't he?" And with that, Dracula lunged at

Tubby's briefs, ripping the elastic. I edged toward the door, and suddenly realized that I was very soon going to be exiting it in one of two ways: (a) on my own power, doing a B.V.D. Advertisement, or (b) on my nekkid posterior, weeping, wailing and gnashing my teeth.

As it turned out, Ancil made my choice for me. It was, thank goodness, Plan (a). Just as Frankenstein and his friends lunged at us, Ancil shoved me out the door, shouting, "Let's get outta here while we've still got our drawers!" And the two of us headed at top speed toward a big oak tree. All the way to the tree, we could hear the snickers of the girls passing by:

"Tee hee, look at Ancil and David!"

"Tsk, tsk, disgraceful and disgusting. I hope a teacher sees them."

"Come on, I think they're kind of cute. Look, they wear different kinds of underwear."

As we reached the protection of the oak tree, I offered up a prayer of thanksgiving for the acorn that had produced it. We looked back in time to see Tubby make his escape from the monsters. He was sprinting toward the high brick wall which surrounded the school, desperately clinging to his undies which had gone from size 40 to about 88 when Dracula tore away the elastic.

Dracula was chasing him, but Tubby climbed onto a bench in an effort to scale the wall. As one leg swung over it, he had to let go of his torn briefs and grab the wall with both hands in order to go over the top. Down went the underwear and up rose the moon as Tubby sort of rolled over the top of the wall and fell safely on the other side. It was the only anti-eclipse of the moon in recorded history ("anti" meaning that instead of disappearing at night, it had *come out* in the middle of the day).

J.E. and Tony came out next, also still in possession of their skivvies, and after scampering back and forth in no particular direction a la the Keystone Kops (sans uniforms), they finally sprinted 100 yards down the length of the football field and waited out the lunch hour beneath the grandstands. They ran the 100-yard dash in record time, and it was a shame they weren't in an official track meet so it could've counted.

Last but not least was Smedley, as the time had arrived for the world's first streak. Ancil and I could hear shouts and screams and cursing and the sounds of much scuffling clear out to our oak tree (which for years after was to be known as "The Tree That Concealed Ancil and David").

Ancil nervously expressed our anxiety for our friend: "The poor guy's in there fighting off ten or twelve of 'em all by himself, and nekkid as a jaybird, too."

"You're not suggesting we go back in the locker room and help him, are you?"

My rhetorical question was made moot as Smedley suddenly came bouncing out the door in his birthday suit, kicking and yelling obscenities from flat on his back.

"Geez, they even got his socks," Ancil muttered.

Smedley hopped up, turned toward the door, shook his fist, and shouted the four words for which he was already famous, but was now to make immortal: "THINK YA FUNNY, HUH?!!!!"

Then Smedley suddenly realized he was standing naked in front of hundreds of people. He became as red as a beet, spun around a couple of times desperately looking for cover and finding none. Finally, he literally and figuratively high-tailed it in the general direction of a picnic table where three coeds and a woman teacher, Miss Lollyberger, were eating their lunch on the sidelines of the football field.

Seeing Smedley rapidly approaching, the coeds screamed and scattered. Miss Lollyberger at first didn't see why they were running, but she arose and trotted after them. After three or four steps, she looked back and, seeing Smedley flying nudely toward the table, exclaimed, "Oh my Lord and His saints preserve us!" and fainted dead away, right there on the fifty-yard line.

Smedley reached the table and deftly turned it onto its side for protection, as sandwiches, chips and cokes flew everywhere. We had seen this table-flipping done by the cowboys in the shoot-em-up western double-feature movies every Saturday for many years, but none of those cowboys ever flipped a table like Smedley did that day.

As he peered over the top to see who had observed his bare-bones scamper, an enormous roar went up from the rapidly gathering crowd—except for Miss Lollyberger, who had quickly recovered and was hurrying off the field. "MORE!!! MORE!!!," everyone shrieked. They couldn't yell "Take it off!" because it was already off. Smedley's repetitious reply was certain, and Ancil and I spoke it to each other as Smedley shouted it to no one in particular: "THINK YA FUNNY, HUH?!!!!"

It had been quite a show, and every one of the spectators had enjoyed it—except, of course, Miss Lollyberger. Smedley had put up an enormous struggle. The locker room was a shambles, and several football jocks sported black eyes and bruises for weeks following Smedley's Last Stand. The coach tried to get him to come out for the team and, failing that, made the guilty monsters run killer laps all week because "A dozen of yew couldn't even subdew a nekkid-as-a-jaybird skinny little eighth grader."

The only thing that marred the purity of Smedley's legendary streak was that it was done against his will. Even so, and there are no ifs, ands, or butts about it, it was the first and the best.

EPILOGUE

In 2004, three young men were arrested for streaking through a fast-food restaurant in Atlanta. They got caught because they had left the motor running in their getaway car and someone stole it, clothes and all. Before their ill-fated scamper, those idiots should've taken a streaking lesson from my pal Smedley, the first of the modern-day streakers. And that's the nekkid truth.

Bill Dill McGill, Almost

That title was almost my name. Mom's maiden name was Dill, and she told me when I was a boy that she almost named me William Dill McGill, or "Bill Dill McGill," and asked me what I would have thought of that.

I was horrified that I had come so close to such a name, and thanked her profusely for not acting on the impulse to bestow such a curse on me. I had already begun to notice the way classmates with funny names were taunted unmercifully by bullies.

But now, at age 66, I think it would've been a fine name once I'd made it through grade school. To this day, the phrase "He's a Dill" or "She's a Dill" has a special, complimentary meaning in my family. It signifies that the person being referred to cares about others and will always "do" for them.

I have always found names fascinating. An interesting thing happened when our daughter Gayle and her husband David were naming their first child. They had picked out a beautiful name, Grace Olivia, for the daughter they were expecting. Just before the birth, however, Gayle realized that together with their last name, Demarest, the child's initials would be GOD. Not wanting to tamper with the name of the Almighty, our granddaughter received the permuted name of Olivia Grace. (But she's still called Grace.)

I always chuckle at the old joke about Joe Piggybristle. Joe hated his name— justifiably—and went to court to get it changed. The judge looked at his name and said, "Joe Piggybristle?!! Whew, I don't blame you. What would you like to change it to?"

Whereupon Joe replied, "JIM Piggybristle. I'm sick and tired of people saying, 'What'cha know, Joe?'!!"

In my teaching career at Georgia Tech, I taught about 5,000 students and got to know every one of them by name. I did this in tribute to one of the best teachers I ever had—Mr. Emby, back at L.S.U. in the late 50s and early 60s. He knew all his students by name, and would call on us in class constantly and unmercifully. I had him for four courses in four separate semesters in the twilight of his career.

During our last semester, Mr. Emby began to have a little trouble remembering some of our names. For example, one day out of the clear blue sky I became "McNeil." But he never forgot an iota of the electrical engineering theory he was imparting to us. One day he wanted to call on my friend Harvey Carruth for an answer, and he said,

"How much is the current in this circuit I've drawn on the board, Mr. Errrrrrr, Ahhhhhhh, Ummmmmmm," and he scratched his head with one hand, boring a hole through Harvey as he pointed the forefinger of his other hand at him. Then he said, "And I'm trying to call on that fella Carruth, but I can't remember his name." Bless his heart, he couldn't figure out why we were laughing.

As we chuckled at the memory lapse, Mr. Emby shook his head in frustration, went to the desk, looked at his gradebook, and said, "CARRUTH! How much is that current, Carruth?" Our names were very important to Mr. Emby, even when he could no longer remember them.

I saw very clearly how much Mr. Emby benefited from his efforts in learning and using our names: We never went to his class unprepared for fear of being embarrassed, so *we studied his material first*. We enjoyed his classes because *we knew he cared about who we were.* We never missed a class because he would pick up that class roll and check attendance mentally every day, and if you missed class the time before, *he would tell you to see him after class and tell him why.* And so on. I vowed that if I were ever to become a teacher, I would emulate his methods, and I'm proud to report that I did.

I had a student once who always ended his signature with an exclamation point, like this: *Arthur Lane!* The first time I saw it, I thought it was just a slip of the pencil, but no, with each and every homework assignment or test the exclamation point was right there in place.

One day Arthur came by during office hours for help, and I said to him, "Arthur, first, tell me about the exclamation point."

His reply was uplifting; he told me he was proud of his name and of who he was, and that he had been using the exclamation point ever since the fourth grade. Back then, his teacher had told him that whenever you saw an exclamation point, it meant that whatever came right before it was interesting, exciting, unexpected, even brilliant. "I wanted to be all those things and make a mark in the world, so I added the exclamation point. It's such a habit now, I guess I'll keep it all my life."

I never saw Arthur again after that class, but I met a man 15 years later who was a teacher, and when he told me where he was from, I said to him that I had once had a student at Georgia Tech from his town by the name of Arthur Lane.

"Oh yes, I remember Arthur," he replied. "He always ended his signature with an exclamation point, and I never knew why." So, I was able to tell him.

That little office-hours session with Arthur made me realize how much college students want to be treated as real people and not just social security numbers, and I was proud that I had followed the example of Mr. Emby and learned—and used—all my students' names.

It's not just students, though, is it? It's all of us who care about our names, whether it's Bill Dill McGill, Joe Piggybristle, Olivia Grace Demarest, Harvey Carruth, or Arthur Lane(!)

"What's in a name?" wrote Shakespeare. The answer is "A LOT." Our names represent who and what we are. From my teacher and my student I learned two things about the importance of names: From my teacher, the benefits of learning, remembering, using and respecting the names of others. From my student, that we should be proud of our names and make a mark in this life so that when we're gone, others will remember us—by our names.

The Teacher with the Stinky Office

A long time ago, I had a brilliant professor for a course in graduate mathematics at L.S.U. I will call him Dr. XYZ; I was reminded of him when I saw the movie *A Beautiful Mind* recently. My professor was not schizophrenic or otherwise mentally ill in any way, to be sure, but he did have his head in the clouds.

He would pace the halls or sidewalks with his hands clasped behind his back, looking upward at the ceiling or the sky, always contemplating the proof of the next great theorem that would bear his name. If you fell in step with him and said, "Professor XYZ? May I ask you a question?", it was always as if you had awakened him from a deep sleep, but he would quickly become alert and be glad to see you and to give you an understandable answer. We really liked him.

I learned a lot in the class I took from Professor XYZ. Several times during the semester I went by his office for help with homework problems and could barely find him, so piled high with books, papers and journals was his desk and floor. To get to the great man, there was actually a little path through the mountain of paper that we had to traverse between the door and a bench beside his chair. I felt like a little rat in a maze, with the professor playing the role of the cheese.

"Mr. McGill, " he said one day as we sat there at his desk, "let me ask you something. Do you detect an offensive odor in this office?"

"Well, yes, Professor, now that you mention it, there *is* a smell in here."

"I would characterize it more as a *stench*," he continued. "Try as I might, I have to date been unable to discover its source. I have had the maintenance people in here, going through the vents and ceiling ducts ad infinitum, and so far the problem has remained intractable. I am convinced that I shall prove Fermat's Last Theorem before I solve the problem of this odoriferous office."

Whenever we graduate students would talk about our classes and profs, the one thing we all agreed on was that if you could find your way to Professor XYZ's desk with a good clothespin firmly affixed to your nose, he could flat teach you some math.

A few years later, I was long gone from L.S.U., and one day I was talking on the phone with a former office-mate of mine who was still there. "Dave," he said, "nobody has proved Fermat's Last Theorem yet, but Professor XYZ's stinky office is no longer an unsolved problem."

"No kidding?"

"Yes. He went to Europe for two years on a sabbatical and, the department being short on space, they got him to clean out his office so that a visiting prof could use it while he was gone."

"And this led to the source of the smell?"

"It did indeed. You'll recall his desk was stacked about three feet high with papers, books, notes, manuscripts, journals and stuff. Well, about halfway down to the wood, in the middle of all that paper he found an old rancid lunch his wife had packed for him. It was evidently fried chicken, deviled eggs and potato salad, and when it was uncovered they practically had to use gas masks to get the office fumigated with opened windows and big box fans."

"Well, my man, I'm glad to hear you folks are getting the really important math problems solved back home," I said.

Out of the Mouth of a Babe

I learned a profound lesson about faith during The Great Atlanta Ice Storm of 1973, when a minor miracle took place in our home.

Our little street was somehow spared the loss of electricity even though the area all around us lost power for the better part of a week. On two of the nearby streets lived two couples—Sal and Jackie, and Bunny and Carol Ann—who to this very day remain four of our most treasured friends, even though they now live in Dallas, Texas and Greensboro, North Carolina. But in 1973 they lived on Meadowcliff and Oakawana, and they and their children moved in with us at the electrified address of 2220 Marann Drive for a week.

The memories we share about those five days are still fresh, even though 30 years have passed and the adults are retired and the nine children are all grown up, most of them with families of their own. Back then we were struggling to find a place in our little house for all of them to sleep, and then getting them bathed and off to bed so the six adults could sneak outside and slide down our neighbor's hilly front yard on an old sled one of the families had brought over.

The next day we spent some time successfully tying off a pine tree that was leaning menacingly over the center of Sal and Jackie's house due to an unbalance of snow and ice. That second night, we cooked hamburgers outside in sub-freezing weather, under a shelter because the storm wasn't quite done with us.

That supper brings to mind a special incident that none of us will ever forget—we still call it The Little Miracle.

The fifteen of us sat down to eat, and we gave thanks for our health, our togetherness, and our food. Then, just as we were finishing the blessing, out went the lights..... And it was as dark as the bottom of the sea.

There was a moment of fearful silence, broken by a tiny voice, that of the youngest child, Kathleen, who bravely and confidently said, "Let's say an Our Father together, and the lights will come back on!"

Omigosh, I thought. Don't say *that*, because then we'll have to pray, and when we're done and the lights are still off, what will all the kids think? It will scar their faith for life. And then all the other children made it worse—in my mind—for their eight little voices echoed as one as they confidently shouted, "YEAH!!! Let's say an Our Father and the lights'll come back on!!!"

So, in spite of my mental reservations, we all launched into The Lord's Prayer.

I would think I had surely dreamed what happened next, except that there were 14 other witnesses. On the last syllable of the prayer—the "men" of "Amen"—the lights flashed back on and the pitchblack room was suddenly as bright as daylight.

What followed became a lifelong lesson to me. The adults, all six of us, were incredulous. We cheered in both amazement and joy at the mini-miracle that had occurred. But when we looked down at the kids, they had already begun to eat their hamburgers. To them, the lights were no miracle...that was what was *supposed* to happen!!

St. Mark wrote (11:24): "Everything you ask and pray for, believe that you have it already, and it will be yours." The children knew those lights were coming on so that they could eat their hamburgers and drink their Cokes, and they didn't bat an eyelash when the room brightened. They had us of little faith outnumbered, 9-6.

We then better understood what Jesus meant when he said, "Let the little children alone, and do not stop them coming to me; for it is to such as these that the kingdom of heaven belongs" (Matthew 19:14). A faith "such as these" is well worth striving for. If the lights are off in your life, it can turn them right back on.

Discovering the Wheel

I was on my way home from work one day when I spotted a huge garage sale in progress. Now normally, there are two reasons why I try to stay away from such things: (1) I believe they are just gimmicks by which people sell their junk so they can go buy other people's junk, and (2) every time I ever stopped at a garage sale, I brought home some of that junk and later regretted it. I'm a terrible shopper.

Garage sale psychology is amazing. Someone should start a course in it in college. I recall when my buddy Sal Calabrese and I were enclosing my garage years ago and I was wondering what in the world I would do with the large old, creaky garage door with a lock that didn't work even before its only key was lost years before.

"The trash men won't haul away anything that size," I said to Sal. "I guess I'll have to pay someone to come and get it and cart it away to the dump."

"Sell it," replied Sal. "People around here will buy *anything*."

Sure enough, I put an ad in the paper for just one weekend and had four people on a waiting list the morning after the ad appeared, wanting to pay good money for that old door. The second guy on the list even insisted on driving to our house with his trailer in case the first fellow didn't show up.

The next day dawned. "Would you take forty bucks?" asked buyer number one, who had arrived ten minutes early. I thought about dickering, with buyer number two due to arrive any minute, but remembered what I had learned from my parents about a bird in the hand and said "Sold!", and away flew my problem. Sal and Jackie and Carolyn and I went out for a fine dinner the next night, courtesy of that old door and Sal's brilliant idea.

Anyway, something prompted me to stop at the aforementioned garage sale, which was enormous. An entire neighborhood was getting rid of its junk over a whole block of tables and garages and front yards. After a few minutes of browsing (you couldn't see it all in a whole day), I thought this would be the first time I stopped at a garage sale and didn't buy anything. But then, as I turned to leave, it caught my eye. Hmmm.

"How much is this thing?" I asked. "Four dollars," the lady said, "and I'll be glad to see it go." At that price, she leaned me a bit. Besides the bargain price, I'd wanted to try one of these ever since the circus came to town when I was a small boy.

But I was also thinking of the downsides: First, it could cost me a fortune in doctor and maybe even hospital bills, and that's probably why she wants to get rid of it. Second, I had heard that the older you get, the more difficult it would be to master it. Third, all my neighbors and friends would surely think I'd lost all my marbles, and in a brand-new neighborhood at that. Finally, there was no way to ascertain whether it even worked or not. I wasn't about to ask that kindly old lady to demonstrate it for me.

Seeing me standing there weighing all the pros and cons, the owner then said, "Oh, heck, give me two bucks." That did it. I bought it. A unicycle. The wheel of death.

I had mastered the three-wheeler when I was a small boy, and a two-wheeler a few years later. And now I was ready, at the prime of my life (37) to try the ultimate: to propel myself forward on one wheel. I was still young enough, I reasoned, to recover and lead a normal life if I landed in the hospital.

Just as I thought, when I arrived home everybody but my adventurous, athletic daughter Gayle thought I was crazy. Gayle has always been a fun-loving person who, like me, will stick with something until she has mastered it. In the case of the unicycle, that takes 50 percent goofiness and 50 percent stubbornness. "Hey! Neat, Dad!! Let's go try it!!!" was her immediate response. And try it we did. And tried. And tried some more...

For about six months we'd go out after work and school and attempt to ride the wheel of death. We took a lot of licks from both the pavement and the unicycle itself. Whenever I fell—which was often—the driveway flailed away at my elbows, hands, and rear end, while the seat and pedals scraped my thighs and shins unmercifully. It brought back memories of pushing off from trees while learning to ride a bicycle 32 years before. But the one-wheeler can go off and leave you much more suddenly and painfully. Plus, my reflexes had slipped a good bit in those decades gone by.

The first thing we learned, therefore, was how to bail out. How to sort of pop off when you know you've lost it and that the little one-wheeled monster has decided to go its own way. And go its own way it does—out the front one time, the back the next, and sometimes off to one side or the other. There is a line in the book of Ezekiel which says, "There was a wheel on the ground by each of them." Old Zeke was quite a prophet when it came to Gayle and me and our unicycle.

Trying to master that thing was incredibly hard work. Somehow the combination of intense concentration and physical effort in trying to "stay afloat" pooped me out after about 20 tries. I was breathing hard with aching legs as if I had been out jogging. But finally, after about three weeks, we reached the point where we could each go about three revolutions, maybe 15 or 20 feet. The tire started getting a little flat and we found that to be a big help as there was much more surface contact for stability.

It took me two weeks to discover that the thing actually had a "front." (The seat was symmetrical.) The pedals kept coming unscrewed, and it finally dawned on me that riding on it one way would keep them tight. That's true on a bike, too, but the problem never arises!

I'm sure that when the wheel was discovered, it wasn't done as it was in the comic strip "B.C." That unicycle doesn't even have pedals; the rider is just standing on the axles (easier to draw?!).

There is an old takeoff on the Beatitudes that goes, "Blessed are those who go around in circles, for they shall be called Big Wheels." A better ending in our case would be "...for they are falling off of a unicycle."

EPILOGUE

Gayle and I succeeded in our quest to master the Wheel of Death, up to a point. We could start at the top of the driveway and ride down the gentle slope all the way to the house, about 50 feet. And we could ride it for a short distance on the flat part of the street. But just as we were poised for complete mastery—that point where you suddenly throw up your hands like Archimedes and yell, "I've GOT IT!!" while riding as far as you want with no more fear or clumsiness—it all ended.

 We left it in the driveway and somebody ran over it, and that was that. I saw another one at another garage sale 13 years later, and this time, at age 50, I said to its owner, "I don't think I could ever get back to where I left off—or rather, fell off, so I don't think so." Good decision, if I do say so myself.

The One and Only "Biggs"
(Eulogy Delivered on November 3, 1999)

I'm Dave McGill, C.J.'s son-in-law.

Charles Joseph Mayeux, Jr. was an American original. I had the pleasure of knowing him for exactly 39 years. We met in the fall of 1960 when his daughter Carolyn invited me home to meet her parents. He made me feel welcome then and thereafter.

In those days he was a plant engineer for a paper mill in St. Francisville, LA. He was a civil engineer from LSU, but his job required him to also function as a mechanical and electrical engineer, purchasing agent, accountant and labor negotiator. C.J. had been promoted there from a mill in Bogalusa, LA, and not long thereafter, following the tragic death of one of his two beloved daughters, Gayle, and the marriage of his remaining child Carolyn to me, he and his wife Vivian accepted a transfer to the west coast where he served as plant engineer at two more mills, first in St. Helen's, Oregon and then in Antioch, California.

During those years C.J. and Vivian began to travel, and over the next 25 years they visited Europe (where C.J. discovered some of his roots and got to use his Louisiana French), as well as Central America, Canada, and all the beautiful parts of the United States. He learned to fly a plane in his sixties (after over a year of hard work getting his blood pressure down so he could qualify medically), and one of the most amazing things I've ever seen was when he and Vivian rented a plane and flew themselves all the way across the country to visit us.

Forced into early retirement in his late fifties, C.J. and Vivian—by this time their grandchildren Michael, Gayle and Meghan had renamed them Biggie and Honey—moved to Florida with very little to their name. But there, Biggie, or Biggs, started over and became a realtor/broker. He also learned to invest and as a result of much hard work, he earned and saved enough to afford himself and Honey a comfortable retirement.

Their last move was to Atlanta nine years ago to be closer to their family, which grew in those last years to include three grandchildren-in-law (Marianne, David and Kevin), and six great-grandchildren: Prosper, Michaela, Grace, Dylan, Cori and Jack. They're all under three years old except Prosper, who will soon be nine, so Biggs was especially close to, and proud of, the little girl he called "Prop". He did a genealogy study and showed her that her gggggggrandfather's name was also Prosper, although in France in 1740 he pronounced it "Pross—PEAR." Their births were exactly 250 years apart.

During these last nine years, Biggs and I became best friends. We ate breakfast together on Saturdays at the Waffle House. We played golf (actually, he played while I hacked), and we were world-class barbequers and martini-makers. He had a million little secrets on how to do things a little better. There was much joke-telling and kidding. I told him he needed to get some miniature jumper-cables in case his pacemaker ever went bad.

With Carolyn and Honey we had jolly, delicious suppers every Wednesday night. We would eat at our house one week, theirs the next, and on the third we would eat at a restaurant. When it was our house's turn, Biggs and I would sit at the piano (neither of us could play, it was just a nice place to prop up the song books), and I would play the banjo and we would sing a few of the "old songs" to warm up for the evening. I think Biggs' favorite was "Ma, She's Makin' Eyes at Me", because it has a line in it that goes "Ma, she wants to marry me, be my Honeybee..." He would get this faraway sparkle in his eyes when he said Honeybee, even though his Honey was right there in the next room.

His love of music went way back. When Carolyn and Gayle were small, back in Bogalusa, all the neighborhood families would get together around a piano and sing and harmonize. Biggs was later to be a charter member of two Barbershop choruses, in Naples and right here in Northeast Atlanta, The Stone Mountain Chorus, which rehearsed right here at Holy Cross Church during the chorus' first 10 years. One thing I'll miss about Biggs is the way he loved the banjo. He played one as a young man in the 30s. He and my little grandson Dylan were the only two people who, when I took out my banjo, would run into the room instead of out of it. I don't know what I'm going to do— Biggs is gone and Dylan's stuck in California.....oh, well.

Over most of this amazing century, Biggs was a hobbyist. He filled a shed with homemade beer as a young man (a rare failure: most of it exploded one muggy summer night), he grafted plants, flew airplanes, built windchimes, made Toastmasters speeches, celestially navigated sail-boats, played excellent golf and bridge, and painted a huge house as a teenager in 1930 to earn money to buy a Model-T car that the sheriff had up for sale for non-payment of taxes. He was a lifelong expert on World War II, which followed from the fact that all three of his siblings served overseas in the conflict—as a soldier, a sailor, and a nurse. Biggs loved to figure out how things work, and possessed an incredibly keen intuition.

Biggs was a fine teacher; he taught me many things and succeeded in his tutelage in all of them except golf. His investment instruction was so successful that I was able to retire this past summer. I had looked forward to being able to spend much more time with Biggs, but I guess God had other plans for us.

Biggs had five devastating crises in his life. Besides the tragic death of Gayle, and the shock of the early retirement, there was a serious hospitalization as a young man after which he quit smoking cold turkey and overcame his ailment. And as a baby, he nearly died when his mother couldn't produce milk and he couldn't keep down anything else they tried. Blessedly, a cousin of one of his parents who was nursing her own baby was well-endowed and took on C.J. as well as her own son for over a year, after which he and Wade Couvillon were forever to refer to each other as—you guessed it—my "bosom buddy."

The last crisis, of course, was Alzheimer's disease, which he battled for the last five years of his life. He never acknowledged it, but instead tried and tried to compensate for his loss of memory and alertness. But he never lost his sense of humor: the day he died, he told the doctor in the hospital his favorite joke, it being about a certain cup of hot coffee in a hospital, which I cannot repeat in a church—but the doctor loved it.

On the way to the hospital in the car, Biggs had noticed on his watch that it was Sunday, and he said to Carolyn and me, "Shouldn't y'all be in church this morning?" I replied that I was sure Father Paul would give us a dispensation for driving an ambulance. He laughed uproariously at that. He hadn't gone to Mass too much in recent months, because he was no longer confident in social situations. Whenever I would tell him he needed to go to Mass and get ready for his final exam, he would laugh and reply that he hoped to be exempted from the test.

A pretty young lady came into the hospital room and said to Biggs, "Mr. Mayeux, I'm your nurse, my name's Amy." He looked at me with a twinkle in his eye, and I knew what he was thinking. "You want to sing her a song, Biggs?" He nodded through the pain, and we launched into "Once in love with Amy, always in love with Amy..." She blushed and said—with a tear in her eye—"Gosh, thank you, my dad used to sing me that a long time ago."

For 61 years of marriage, Biggs brought his beloved Honey coffee in bed every morning. That was a lot of coffee, about 23,000 cups. Doubling it for their second cups, it came to 46,000, and always sweetened with a lot of love.

We miss this man of great integrity, loyalty, diligence and humor, as we give thanks for his magnificent life.

What Was John's Password

I own a tape of perhaps the funniest sketch of all time—Abbott and Costello's old "Who's on First" routine. In case you've never heard it, in the interchange Abbott is the manager of a baseball team. The first baseman's name is "Who", the second baseman is "What", and "I Don't Know" is on third. Costello is trying to find out who the players are, and a small bite of the dialogue goes like this: C: What's the guy's name on first base? A: He's on second. C: I'm not asking you who's on second. A: Who's on first. C: I don't know. A: He's on third.

And on and on it would go, rapid-fire, with poor Costello becoming more and more frustrated...

When students started using computers at Georgia Tech, my professor buddy Bob Shreeves became the Computer Coordinator for our department. One of his duties was to assign passwords for students who wished to use the school's computer. Passwords were only semi-secret then, and students didn't have their own PCs. Bob liked to make up silly passwords. His own password was "That."

One day I was sitting in Bob's office; before we could go to lunch, he had to wait for student John Whatley to come by for his password. Bob asked me what I thought would be a good password for Whatley.

"What," I replied.

"What would be a good password for Whatley?" Bob asked me again.

"Yes," I answered. And Bob caught on without my having to explain my little joke. He gave me a wink, and replied with his famous grin.

"You're doing a little Abbott and Costello on me, aren't you, Dave?"

"Yep."

So, when John knocked on Bob's door a few moments later, here's how the interchange took place:

JW: "Dr. Shreeves, what's my password?"

Bob: "Yes."

JW: "What?"

Bob: "That's right."

JW: "What's right?"

Bob: "Yes, it is. That's it."

JW: "That's my password?"

Bob: "No, no, no. That's my password. What is *your* password."

JW: "Sir, if I knew it, I wouldn't be asking you what it is."

Bob: "NOW you've got it."

JW: "I've got what?"

Bob: "That is correct."

JW: "What is correct?"

Bob: "Absolutely."

JW: "Dr. Shreeves, let's try something else. What's *your* password?"

Bob: "No, John, what is *yours*."

JW: "I asked you first."

Bob: "And I told you."

JW: "Told me what?"

Bob: "Yes, mine is that, and yours is what."

JW: "Your what is that and my which is what? Aaarrrggggghhhh, never mind. Look, Dr. Shreeves, I have to go now. But when that computer machine asks me to type in my password, what do I type?"

Bob: "Yep!"
JW: "What?"
Bob: "You got it."
JW: "On the contrary, I think I've *had* it."

The Free Spirits Made John Roll on the Floor

All my life I had heard the expression "rolling on the floor laughing," and wondered why anyone had thought up such a silly way of describing uproarious laughter. I mean, I had seen (through the window) Holy Rollers rolling on the floor of a little church in prayer, and I had seen (on the movie screen) cowboys rolling on the floor to get out of the line of fire of the crooks, but never had I seen anyone rolling on the floor laughing. And when my mama's family got together, we laughed a lot.

One night, though, I finally saw it happen, but it'll take me a little while to set the scene for you.

I love barbershop harmony, the pure sound of four voices blending a cappella to sing an old-time American song in true pitch. For eight years, I was the tenor in a quartet called "The Free Spirits." We would practice one night a week in our homes, taking turns, and about once a month we would "sing out" in churches, prisons, hospitals, anniversary celebrations, fundraisers, nursing homes, shopping centers, conventions, weddings, retreats, shows, and even several times at a monastery.

Don Waller sang lead, Gus Ghirardini handled bass, and Tom Schlinkert was our baritone. We got along great, which was essential for a quartet's longevity. And we had—if I do say so myself—a really good sound.

We had a lot of fun, made a lot of people happy, and it was a great experience. When we were ready for our closing song, one of our standard jokes was to say, "Well, we're going to do our encore now, because we've been fooled too many times in the past!"

In 1980, along with Bill Shreiner, Larry Crabbe and a number of other enthusiastic voices, our quartet formed the Stone Mountain Chorus, a new chapter of SPEBSQSA (The Society for the Preservation and Encouragement of Barbershop Quartet Singing in America). The chorus is going strong—now in its 25th year—but, frankly, it caused The Free Spirits to fizzle away because of all the work involved in organizing it.

My fondest memory of my quartet is not that we performed before a thousand people at a show in the Atlanta Civic Center or in front of tens of thousands at an Atlanta Braves game, both of which we did. It was, instead, the four of us singing a song in my neighbors' living room for just the two of them, sitting on their sofa.

In barbershop, the songs always end with a "tag," which is a last line of ringing chords which, for those of us who love it, sends one chill after another right up your spine. Most barbershoppers like to stand around sometimes and, bypassing the songs, just sing one tag after another.

Now The Free Spirits had a tradition. After a couple of hours of rehearsal, we would have coffee and cake, then whoever was the the host would walk the other three members out to their cars and on the front lawn we would sing four tags, each of us choosing one.

Gus would often pick the tag to "The Sunshine of Your Smile" because it began with the bass alone singing the words "Your smile..." with two notes that were way, way down low. Tom frequently chose a challenging, lengthy tag that was a combination of Stephen Foster songs such as "Camptown Races" and "Ring, Ring the Banjo." My favorite tag was "While Sweet Dreams Rest You, Dear Old Pal." And you never knew what tag Don was going to pick—he liked them all. But one thing was sure: When we belted out those four tags, we definitely woke up the neighborhood.

Now in those days Carolyn and I had a delightful couple named John and Ann for neighbors. They were fond of barbershop, and whenever they noticed that the quartet was practicing next door, they would come out on their porch and listen to the tags as Gus, Tom and Don were departing. I didn't even know they were eavesdropping until one night when, after the tags, they applauded and yelled out for more. We got to talking with them, and they asked us to sing a whole song for them. The next thing you know, we were in their living room with them on their couch, ready for the performance. Four guys singing for an appreciative audience of two.

We were quite famous for this one song that was sung to the tune of the old singalong standard "Side By Side." It was about this poor fellow who, on his wedding night, was shocked instead of thrilled as his wife got ready for bed. She took off her wig (revealing a bald head beneath), her teeth, one eye, one arm and one leg, and, one-by-one, placed them on a chair. The last three lines of the song went like this:

> *I stood there broken-hearted.*
> *MOST OF MY WIFE HAD DEPARTED.*
> *So I slept on the chair —*
> *There was MORE OF HER THERE,*
> *Side by side.*

We had always gotten a great response to the song before, but it was nothing like that night in front of John and Ann. Before we even got to the punchlines, John was laughing so hard he was crying, and so loud that we were having trouble hearing one another. And he was starting to slide down in his seat, and banging his open hands against his thighs in glee.

And then it happened, the only time I've ever seen it in my life. When we sang "Most of my wife had departed," his slide ended on the floor as he laughed uproariously all the louder, rolling over and over and banging the floor with his open palms. And Ann was laughing more at John than she was at the song.

Right about then, we lost it. It was the only time in our eight years that we couldn't finish a song. Oh, we finished it, but truth be told, it was just an effort on the last two lines to laugh in four-part harmony because we were cracking up so gleefully that we couldn't get the words out. After John recovered, we sang the last three lines over, and he started laughing again and so did Ann and so did we.

In my entire life, that was the loudest and longest I ever laughed.

Remembering Uncle Albert

When I became the founding director of The Center for the Enhancement of Teaching and Learning (CETL) at Georgia Tech in December 1986, I was talking about this new responsibility with my father-in-law, C.J., over the Christmas holidays.

"I wish there were some easy way to begin helping faculty to improve their communications skills," I said. "Something I could do that wouldn't take a long time to plan and execute, so we could hit the ground running when I take office in the new year. Something that would be fun."

C.J.'s reply was to make a huge difference in several hundred (and counting) Tech faculty and staff. "You know, Dave, you might consider a Toastmasters club. I belonged to one for three years during my time on the West Coast, and it helped me immeasurably in my ability to give talks and speeches."

Bingo. That was just the sort of thing I was looking for, and it was great to learn that the wheel had already been invented. There was a Toastmasters club across the street from Tech at Coca Cola's international headquarters, and it became our sponsoring club. We were soon off and running. We called our club "Techmasters" and as I write this, it's 17 years old and still going strong. I estimate that in those 17 years I have listened to close to 2000 speeches covering just about every subject under the Sun, so I've learned a lot at Techmasters—as well as had a great time with many friends.

I have one personal story to relate concerning speechgiving at Techmasters. One year, we got interested in telling tall tales, and had a club contest to see who could tell the biggest "fish story." A tall tale is a yarn that is clearly untrue (and is even ridiculous), but which is written with great imagination and told with such sincerity that the audience "almost believes it."

Now Toastmasters holds four contests a year at levels higher than the individual club; these are the humorous speech, the serious (usually motivational) speech, the tall tale, and the evaluation contest. Our club had rarely been interested in these; the members were much too busy, and we just used our club as a once-a-week workshop to improve our skills and that was it.

But that year of the tall tale, I wanted to test mine at a higher level, so I took it to the Area Contest, which comprised the best tall tales from all the clubs in one's area of the city. (The winner would go further, to the Division Contest, comprising the best tales from a division of the state, in my case Georgia.)

I came in second. I was miffed—not because I lost, but because the winner just stood up there and told a bunch of one-liners—jokes which weren't even related. And I had told this marvelous (in my opinion, of course) tall tale.

The next year, I entered my tale again. Same result, another second place to another winner who just told unrelated jokes. And if you can believe it, I tried it one last time a year later, and the same thing happened for the third year in a row. I was feeling like Avis, ever number two and trying harder. But this time something fortuitous occurred. The person who won the Area Contest had a conflict and couldn't compete in the Division Contest and so it devolved upon me to represent my Area.

I knew now that my tall tale would at last and at least get a fair hearing, because at the higher levels, the judges know a good tall tale when they hear one. And indeed, I won the Division Contest and in so doing reached the "finals," which was the District Contest for the best tall tale in the State of Georgia.

At District, there were six Division winners competing. I placed third, losing to a pair of pretty wild tales, and felt great about it. But before retiring my story, it was to get one more hearing. I heard about the Atlanta History Center's annual Lying Contest, which was another tall tales exhibition. You sent in your tale on tape, and the best ten were invited to the annual conference at which the Lying Contest provided the main entertainment. Mine was selected as one of the ten.

There was an interesting requirement placed on the tales in the Lying Contest, which was that each of them had to end with the same sentence. In my year, that sentence was "And that's when I quit." As you'll see, I only had to alter my tale slightly to get to that closing line; otherwise it was the same as I had presented in the various Toastmasters contests. I called my story "Remembering Uncle Albert." Here it is; see if you believe it:

Albert Einstein was actually my uncle by marriage. I only saw him once, when I was a small boy. He was touring the South, and stopped briefly to visit—for the first and only time—with his in-laws.

I'll always remember his wild frizzy hair, his baggy clothes and his pipe, and especially his smile and his dreamy eyes as he leaned over to me and my six cousins and said in his marvelous German accent, "Now kiddies, don't you effer forget dat nutting in der vorld can travel fashter den der shpeed uff light."

I'm sure he said some other things, but that statement about the speed of light is all I can recall. The reason it's so vivid in my mind is surely because of the profound impact it made on a little 5-year-old like me in 1944. So much so, that I began to experiment with the speed of light to see if Uncle Albert was correct in his thinking.

Alas, I began to realize that Uncle Al was all wet! For over the next few years, I began to break the speed of light in all kinds of ways. First, I practiced and practiced until I could switch off the light at the wall switch of my room at night, and SSHHHHHHHHHHHOOOOOOOOOOM, I'd be across the room and into my bed and under the covers before the light went out! (I can't do this any more because of all my creaky joints, which is the only thing in this story that's not true!)

And when my mother wasn't around, I'd go into the kitchen and, repeatedly, I would yank open the door of the refrigerator, faster and faster and faster until I was doing it so fast that I could look inside and see darkness for an instant before it flashed into light! Things were not looking good for Uncle Albert.

Another thing I could do after much practice was to run out of the house in the middle of the day so fast that I could look all around me on the ground and see nothing, and then watch with glee while the Sun laid down my shadow.

I still remember vividly the last time I broke the speed of light. It was late afternoon on a sunshiny day in May. I was outside doing a chore, and my brother Dinky was taunting me with all kinds of insults. He wanted me to hit him, because my Dad had told me, "Now look here, if I see you hit your brother one more time, you will be grounded for the entire summer. That means no listening to the radio, no picture shows [now known as movies], no baseball and no ice cream for three months. Do you understand that, son?" I did, so I was trying hard to be good.

But Dinky was trying equally hard to be BAD. He wanted that grounding to take place, and he was picking on me unmercifully. And finally I had had enough and I swung a punch at him. And to my horror, with my fist in mid-air, I glanced across the yard and there in the driveway was my Dad, home from work and getting out of his car, and looking right at me.

I knew I was a dead man, or rather a dead boy..........UNLESS!! Unless I could get to Dad's side before the ray of light got there that would bring to his eyes the image of me hitting Dinky. It was my only hope. I had to try it; it was too late to stop the punch.

So, POW! I clobbered Dinky and SHHHH-HHHHHHOOOOOOOOOOOOMMM, I flew to Dad's side and looked back, and realized I had made it, because—Hallelujah!—I saw myself across the yard hitting my brother.

My dad looked down at me, scratched his head, and said, "Hello, David. You know, I've got to get my glasses checked because I could've sworn I just saw you over there across the yard punching Dinky like I warned you not to do. But that can't be, because you're standing right here beside me."

"Maybe you've just been working too hard, Dad," I replied. "Come on inside, and I'll fetch your slippers and pipe and the newspaper while you relax before dinner."

He thanked me and we went into the house, and I realized I had dodged what would've been a very painful bullet.

After that incident, I began to think seriously about Uncle Albert. If word got out that I was routinely shattering the speed of light, it would destroy his stupendous career. His whole life would be ruined, and for what purpose, anyway? Also, I was getting tired of all the hard work involved in breaking the speed of light…And that's when I quit.

Of the ten finalists, my tall tale was the fifth one given. The large crowd loved it, and I knew I was #1 so far. I also felt that my story had it all over numbers 6, 7, 8, and 9 as they followed in turn. But alas, the tenth speech blew everybody away. The teller was masterful and he had the audience, myself included, in stitches as he told of the hilarious day a tornado ripped through his town. Even with a penalty for going overtime, he won easily.

I placed second, but since the winner had come down from Tennessee for the contest, they told me that for the next year I could consider myself "The Biggest Liar in Georgia."

I haven't written any more tall tales. That's when I quit.

Trung Nguyen's Escape

I first met Trung Nguyen in the winter of 1985 when he came into my Dynamics class and lit up the room with his big smile. Over the next 10 weeks, he proved to be a very good student, excelling not only in learning the difficult subject matter, but also in his attitude, attendance, participation and effort. A few times, when he was stumped by homework problems, he came to my office for help. Always courteous and appreciative, he epitomized the kind of student we professors dearly love to teach, for this young Vietnamese has always loved to learn.

He was born in October of 1961 in Saigon, the first of nine children. They lived in that big city for five years. Trung has one particularly vivid memory of those years, that of his mother taking him to Hung Vuong Hospital to get treatment for his polio and to pick up a pair of special shoes. He remembers long, painful days of therapy — exercises and walking with his mother to strengthen the muscles in his legs. Because of those struggles, he gets around quite well today.

In 1966, Trung's family moved 370 miles north to Nha Trang, in a hilly area near the sea. His father was a policeman; his mother, a housekeeper. For the next five years, though war and death raged across his country, the area in which he lived was fairly secure. He remembers American soldiers coming to the town as friends, and that most of them left in 1973.

In May 1975 Trung's family returned to Saigon, which had fallen one month earlier to the communists. Trung was left in Nha Trang with friends to complete the school year. A month later, he gave his only possession, a bicycle, to a friend and rode a bus to Saigon to join his family. Then nearly 14 years old, he found his family sharing a small, old house and barely scraping by, fixing and selling used bicycles. Trung remembers that a huge windfall occasionally occurred in which they might sell a bike for $20 more than they had paid for it; this would feed the large family for nearly a week.

They spent a year in Saigon, during which time Trung's father spent several weeks in a re-education camp. They then moved to Rach Gia, a village near the Cambodian border. Mr. Nguyen became a rice farmer and barber, but Trung remembers that the time they spent there was miserable for his family—far worse than selling bikes in Saigon. They were constantly having to sell their belongings, piece by piece, just to survive.

Trung completed the equivalent of high school as a superior student, but recalls the anguish he felt when his applications for college-level study were denied time and time again by the new regime. He committed himself to the goal, if it took a lifetime, of gaining two things: education and freedom. To obtain them, the teenager knew he must escape.

To buy help, Trung saved several hundred dollars, but was ripped off by people who took the money and then reneged on their promise to help him flee. Undaunted, he started saving again, working as a locksmith, a farmer, and, as always, a repairer of bicycles. This time, he did not give up the money until he was on the boat, along with 24 others. He took nothing with him but the money and a compass.

There was a close call with a Vietnamese government patrol boat early on, but the escape boat outran it—barely.

Trung's elation was short-lived, however, when everyone realized that their vessel leaked and the outboard motor ran when it felt like it (which was seldom). For these reasons, the next two days were the worst of Trung's life. There was no food or drinking water, and the refugees spent more than two days pouring salty water over their parched bodies and bailing out the boat as it slowly traversed 70 miles toward a rendezvous with a fishing vessel from Bangkok. All 24 of Trung's companions survived the ordeal because, as he put it, "We all had *resolution.*"

Trung said the occupants of the fishing boat were "not pirates, but very close." They took everything, even Trung's compass, but the fact that they had water, food, a seaworthy vessel, and a destination of Thailand was worth any price to Trung and his fellow refugees.

Next came five long months in three refugee camps in Thailand, each one inching him ever closer to freedom. At the last camp, Panat Nikhom, Trung learned that he had been accepted to emigrate to America. His last stop was a four-month stint in Bataan, in the Philippines. In December of 1981, he finally arrived in Atlanta, having lived out the line to Neil Diamond's song:

"On the boats and on the planes, they're coming to America."

The International Rescue Commission (IRC) helped Trung find a modest apartment, and after three weeks of orientation and job-hunting he went to work as a janitor. Six months later, he passed the English proficiency exam on the first try. After saving some money, he entered DeKalb Community College in the winter of 1983. At the same time, he went to work for the IRC part-time, working with refugees and repaying the kindness he had received.

Trung transferred to Georgia Tech in the fall of 1984, and on Sept. 4, 1987, after three years of hard work and with a B-average, he received a bachelor's degree in electrical engineering. Throughout those years, Trung ran the IRC Refugee House for Vietnamese immigrants, finishing off what he called his "freedom debt."

Parallel to his studies at Tech and his work with the refugees from his homeland, Trung burned the midnight oil, learning more and more about this strange land that had embraced him, preparatory to becoming a citizen. Just as with his technical studies, everything was accomplished in record time—temporary resident, permanent resident, citizenship applicant and, on June 12, 1987, Trung pledged allegiance to the United States of America.

Five months after leaving Vietnam, Trung established communications with his family, and they have corresponded monthly for the past six years. At a Fourth of July cookout at our home, he told my wife Carolyn and me how much he missed them all, but that he was happy with the decision he had made back in Rach Gia. He said, "I wished for two things—freedom and education. In this year, I have obtained them both. I have become a citizen of a free land, and have received a college degree." Later, he entertained us with piano, guitar and folk songs of his past and present. He regularly does this for Vietnamese-Americans at his church, the Second Ponce de Leon Baptist.

One of the most rewarding things about teaching at Tech is that we get to meet people like Trung, whose next goal is to use his Ramblin' Wreck sheepskin to find an engineering job. He was looking forward to interviews as he patiently continues to work with new refugees from all over the world.

§

I wrote the above story in 1987. Now it is 2005, and Trung has just left my home after a New Year's visit. Let me fill you in on Trung's past 18 years with a sequel to his story:

After graduation, Trung went to work for Occidental Chemical Co. in Muscle Shoals, Alabama. While there, he regularly sent money from each paycheck to his family back in Vietnam while he saved and planned to bring them to America.

In 1991 Trung changed jobs, moving to Air Products Corporation in Pensacola, Florida. He has advanced since then to the position of Principal Engineer in Instrumentation and Electrical Engineering.

Trung's goal of bringing his family to a better life than living under the Communism which had enveloped their country was ultimately fulfilled in April 1992 when his mother, two sisters and five brothers joined him in their new land.

Six of the seven siblings are now married; they live in Florida, South Carolina, Indiana and Utah. Trung's mother lives in a home he bought for her in Pensacola.

During all the time following graduation, Trung had a dream of marriage and a family. He had his former pastor in Atlanta on the lookout for a potential bride and, in 1996, Trung got the call which told him his pastor had found a beautiful prospect, inside and out. Trung and Ngoc were married the next year, and Carolyn and I were pleased to be the only non-Vietnamese in attendance.

Trung and Ngoc have two lovely children, Rebecca and Jonathan. At the aforementioned New Year's visit, these two tiny children each sang "Silent Night" for Carolyn and me, unaccompanied and in perfect pitch. Their little voices capped off our Christmas/New Year's season and brought tears of joy to our eyes.

Only in America. What a country.

A Batty Experience

In the summer of 1992, mosquitos were amazingly absent from our yard. What with a creek along the back of the property, and a neighbor on the other side of said creek who was constantly sucking it nearly dry with a pump to water his lawn—causing the creek to remain stagnant and breed mosquitos—it was more than passing strange that the little vampires seemed to be taking a summer off.

We delighted in sitting out back on the swing every day between dusk and dark, taking in the pleasant night air while retaining our blood.

Then one day in midsummer, I was on the top floor of our home when I heard a scratching sound coming from just above the attic fan loovers. I climbed up there to investigate and found, to my surprise, a little bat. That attic fan area was the only place such a creature could've survived in the attic with all the insulation we had had blown in up there.

I scooped up the little fellow and kept it in a box until dark, when upon release outside, it gratefully flew away. But by then, I had put two and two together, and I returned to the attic. Shining a flashlight against the end of the house, I saw about three dozen bats literally and figuratively hanging out; they were dangling from a large triangular screen that separated the attic from a louvered wooden gable vent. Together with its twin on the other end of the house, these vents allowed air to flow the length of the house, through the attic. My adventurous little bat had squeezed through a spot where one of the screen's staples had come loose.

Now a single bat can eat more than 600 mosquitos in a mere hour of dining, so the conundrum of our mosquitoless yard had been solved. The bats nesting at our house alone were gobbling up almost 22,000 skeeters per hour every night. Nonetheless, as I approached the screen from the attic, it was clear that the bats had to go. Their guano and urine didn't smell so good, to say it mildly, and the droppings had begun to spill over onto the insulation, meaning it wouldn't be long before it started staining the sheetrock on the bedroom ceilings.

I didn't relish the thought of becoming a landlord brandishing an eviction notice: "I'm sorry, but you folks will have to leave. You're behind on your rent and you're driving me batty." But the house had to come first.

I did some research and found out how to do the eviction humanely. It's called "screening them out."

One night, while most of the bats were out eating mosquitos, my friend Scott Spinner got in the attic with a water pistol and a flashlight, and squirted the few bats that weren't out for dinner. They hate that, and quickly flew away. When Scott called out that the screen was batless, I climbed up a ladder outside with a pre-prepared second screen and tacked it over the outside of the loovers. That wasn't easy: the loovers are about 12 feet wide and two feet high, and nearly 30 feet off a sloping ground. But we got it done.

We then put up three bat houses close by, but the bats were having none of it. They were far too insulted by their eviction to accept alternative housing anywhere near our premises.

And, of course, back came the "skeeters" with a vengeance, and, alas, they've been here ever since.

Carolyn, R.N.

To our grandkids: Your grandmother became a nurse when she was 44 years old. Truth be told, she had already been a nurse for 22 of those years, because all moms who raise children, caring constantly for their physical and mental well-being, have to be nurses—the good old practical kind.

Carolyn paid all the usual dues, mending the scrapes, cuts and bruises and hurt feelings, and driving the kids to doctors' offices and hospitals all those years. But her interest went much farther. A fan of medicine, she has always soaked up knowledge of the subject like a sponge. Several of her doctors have observed her knowledge and sensed her caring interest, and offered her unsolicited jobs in their offices.

When she was 41, Carolyn was doing volunteer work at a retirement home. She was biding her time, waiting hopefully to be accepted for a hospital counseling program. When the program was postponed, she became discouraged and told her mother, Vivian, about her disappointment one day while they were out for a walk.

"Well then, Carolyn, why don't you try for something bigger?" asked her mother, a nurse in her younger years.

"What do you mean?"

"Go to school and become a nurse. If I could do it, you can surely do it. Anyway, that's what you've always wanted to be, isn't it?"

"Well, yes, I have thought of it, but I could never pass the math, and besides, I'd be 44 years old by the time I became a nurse in three years."

Vivian gave her a perfect reply: "How old will you be in three years if you *don't* become a nurse?"

"What about the math?" Carolyn was rapidly running out of excuses.

"Nothing to it. Dave can help you through it."

And that did it. Back to college went Carolyn, full of optimism tempered by a few doubts.

I, the teacher, was soon recruited to be the math tutor. It was a tough assignment, but we got through it as Carolyn passed the math as well as everything else with flying colors.

What she did was pursue a dream. She looked out the window and instead of merely admiring the rainbow, she followed it to its end. She found there a pot of gold, and the gold that was in it comprised the tools and skills of the nurse she became.

But Carolyn soon found that her troubled feet and back wouldn't allow her to perform the rigors of full-time floor nursing. So she worked as a medications nurse at a retirement home for a while. Then she did private duty nursing for a couple of years, and after that she taught a number of wellness classes at two churches in our area.

Finally, she retired from formal nursing. But through the years since then, she has given good advice, when asked, to countless friends and relatives about their medical problems, including me.

Carolyn's accomplishment reminds me of two lines from Roger Whittaker's great song "New World in the Morning":

I met a man who had a dream he's had since he was twenty;
I met that man when he was eighty-one.....

You're never too old to pursue a dream.
Go for it!

The Card Maker

Every day I say a very brief poetical prayer:
"Thank you, God, for my life and my wife."
Of course, inherent in that sentence of gratitude is an expression of deep appreciation to my parents for the "life" part of the prayer. As to the "wife" part: At this writing I've been married to her—Carolyn—for 44 years.

She never had a middle name. Born close to Christmas, her mother thought that "Carolyn" was both appropriate and beautiful and that a middle name would therefore be superfluous.

That middle-nameless decision did cause some problems for our heroine, however. At LSU (where I met her in 1960), she wrote "None" in the space for her middle name at freshman registration, and so for four years she appeared in the campus directory as "Carolyn None Mayeux."

Nowadays, however, Carolyn has lots of names. Her Godmother called her Cally, and a few friends call her Caroline. Four of her grandchildren know her as Gie-Gie (rhymes with ME-me), and a fifth calls her Granny Carolyn. The sixth and oldest, Prosper, calls her Grandmerry. Carolyn once asked Prosper, "Why do you call me 'GrandMary'? My name isn't Mary." Prosper replied, "It's not GrandMary, it's GrandMERRY, because you're always smiling! M-E-R-R-Y!!"

But by any other name, and to me, she's The Card Maker.

Years ago, Carolyn began recycling old greeting cards, photos and artwork, using them to create beautiful new cards for friends and family. She further decorates them with old lace, bird feathers, wallpaper scraps, ribbons, watercolor, and gorgeous self-pressed flowers. And lately, she's dusted off her old sewing machine so she can incorporate little sections of antique quilts, stitching them into some of her cards. So each card is obviously unique.

One day Carolyn even asked me to save her a drawing from a company's annual report to stockholders, which was a silhouette of a number of children holding hands and walking happily along. It became the focal point of an exquisite card.

The Card Maker always stays far ahead, making between four and eight cards at a sitting—usually late at night—and keeping those as yet unsent in a large basket in her "card room." It is a joyful room, because it shares space with the multitude of toys our grandkids love to get into.

Most days when I come down to fix my morning coffee there will be two or three of the cards in addressed envelopes ready to head for the post office to bring a greeting of pleasure to the lucky recipient. Sometimes they're for birthdays, or for illnesses, sympathy, recollections, retirements or other congratulatory occasions, encouragement, or just "thinking of you" messages.

I am very proud to be married to The Card Maker. Years ago, with my cartooning I used to think I was the artsy one in the family, but I know better now.

Musings on the Banjo

I don't remember the first time I heard a banjo, but I recall vividly the day I first bought one. I'll tell you how it came to pass.

There was a "Folk Mass" movement sweeping the Catholic church in America in the 60s, and our musical pastor, Msgr. Michael Regan, recruited a few parishioners to play guitars and lead the singing at such a liturgy in our parish. I was one of the volunteers.

The Monsignor appointed Fr. Jim Sexstone to say the folk mass each week. The Mass, held in the cafeteria, was well-attended, and Fr. Jim's homilies were marvelous. He would bring in a comic strip from the Sunday funnies— usually it was "Peanuts"—and craft a sermon around it. And he had the amazing ability to do this week after week in such a way as to captivate both the children and the adults.

The quality of the music, however, was not keeping pace with that of the homilies. For a few months there, four of us were all trying to learn to play the guitar. And there was a guy tooting on a recorder with which we could never seem to get in tune, and a number of other problems. And Msgr. Regan, God rest his soul, was only finicky about one thing in his life: the music in his parish.

At first, he didn't trust us to lead the singing, and so he staggered the starting times of the masses: 10:00 in the church and 10:15 in the cafeteria. That way, he could lead the opening song in the church and quickly dash across the parking lot for the opening song in the cafeteria. Back he would scamper to the church for the Offertory song, then he'd hustle back to the cafeteria, and so on. This went on for a couple of months until cold weather suddenly blew in one Sunday, and after slipping on the ice in the parking lot while dashing to the cafeteria for the Communion song, he told us, "I think you folks can handle it now."

Putting us in charge didn't make us any better, however, and one day at rehearsal Fr. Jim said, "You know, I think if one of you would take up the banjo, it would add some spice to the music." I volunteered, and one Saturday he and I went to a number of pawn shops and music stores and found a banjo which I bought and began to learn to play.

It did indeed add spice, and immediately so. And it was the banjo, not me, that did it. I got some picks, learned just a few basic chords and rolls, and the way the notes would dance along atop the strummed chords of the guitars just seemed to add happiness to the music of Joe Wise and Ray Repp and Sister Miriam Therese Winter. To this day, nearly 40 years later, people will tell me how they fondly remember those Masses in the cafeteria (and later in the gymnasium) and they'll say, "...And you played the banjo."

Yes, I did, or at least I tried to, and for nearly forty years the banjo has brightened my days. The banjo I ended up with for my retirement years has a long neck. I love things with long necks—the Mississippi River (where in 1961 on a ferry halfway across, Carolyn said she'd marry me), giraffes, beer in long-necked glass bottles, my Aunt Laura (God rest her soul), and, especially, my banjo. Pete Seeger invented the long-neck 5-string banjo when he realized that by adding three more frets high up on the neck, he could more easily play songs in the keys of E, F, and F-sharp. It was a stroke of genius, because lots of songs are best sung in those keys.

Banjos are truly instruments of happiness, best illustrated by the four panels of an old Peanuts comic strip in which Linus is musing to Charlie Brown:

"I feel sorry for little babies...

"When a little baby is born into this cruel world, he's confused! He's frightened!

"He needs something to cheer him up...

"The way I see it, as soon as a baby is born, he should be issued a banjo!"

In that one little piece of art, the late great Charles Schulz personified the power of the banjo to lift the spirit.

And yet, sadly, the banjo doesn't bring happiness to everyone. People are rarely ambivalent about the sound of the banjo. They either love it or they don't. You can find a plethora of jokes on the internet denigrating the banjo. One of the cruelist is:

"You know the difference between a banjo and an onion?"

"No, what is it?"

"Nobody cries when you chop up a banjo."

Then there's an old "Far Side" cartoon that depicts an orchestra conductor yelling angrily, "STOP! STOP!! WHAT'S THAT SOUND? WHAT'S THAT SOUND??!" And if you look carefully, you see a funny-looking fellow amidst the violins and other fine instruments plunking away on a banjo. You're supposed to wonder along with the conductor how that barbaric twang got in there, I suppose.

I have very mixed feelings about such put-downs of the banjo. I consider myself an amateur humorist and cartoonist, and in that role I find the onion joke and the orchestra cartoon really funny. But as an advocate of the banjo, they also make me sad. Lovers of the banjo, like Linus and me, wish that everyone could discover the joy in the banjo as we have.

I've experienced banjo discrimination first-hand. Let me describe it using a line about how Cajuns love their hunting dogs. In an old story, a Cajun says, "Now look here, you can talk 'bout my wife, my mother, my kids, my house, my job, my car, but don't you say a word about my huntin' dog, you hear?" There is a similarly fierce loyalty among lovers of the banjo. Once I was in a folk group and the leader asked me to do more singing and less banjo playing on most of the songs. I was probably thinking, "You can talk about my huntin' dog, but don't you talk about my banjo!", because I took offense, left, and never went back.

Of course, on the other side of the banjo divide, there have been many more praises sung to the banjo than just the Peanuts cartoon. One fine literary tribute is an 1894 poem by Rudyard Kipling, "The Song of the Banjo," in which the banjo itself tells its story, and lauds its portability, particularly in wartime. After a few lines dismissing pianos, fiddles and organs as impossible to survive in a military campaign, the banjo says:

> "I travel with the cooking pots and pails —
> I'm sandwiched 'tween the coffee and the pork —
> And when the dusty column checks and tails,
> You should hear me spur the rearguard to a walk."

The banjo came to America from Africa. Early on, it comprised gut strings, a carved neck, and a possum hide stretched over a gourd. Before long, they were manufactured, and in the 1800s there were upwards of a million banjos in the expanding U.S., with one in nearly every home in the midwest. But then it almost died out—especially the 5-string version—only to re-emerge when Earl Scruggs popularized his three-finger bluegrass style in the middle of the last century.

My own playing and singing really began in 1964, when I was 25. Mrs. Santa Claus gave me a ukelele for Christmas during our three years in Kansas. She has an excellent ear, and tuned it to "My dog has fleas" in seconds. I learned some chords, and was soon playing and singing some simple songs.

Now comes the embarrassing part. The next Christmas, I graduated to a guitar. It came with a record that purported to teach me how to tune it. But the man on the record didn't know how dumb at least one of his students might be. The first and sixth strings on a guitar are both tuned to "E" a couple of octaves apart. The voice was instructing me to tighten the first string to a certain high sound, and I was obediently doing just that to what seemed like the first string to me—the one that was closest to my brain, anyway.

Sadly, that string was the sixth, not the first, and about halfway from the low to the high "E" it broke with a loud pop and flew up and drew a little blood from my forehead. I was so embarrassed and disappointed that I slipped the guitar under the bed and didn't touch it again for three years, when we had moved to Georgia and Msgr. Regan was recruiting his volunteers.

Most of what I learned about the banjo is in the distant past. For most of my adult life I've been coasting along, using the banjo to accompany singing for friends and family and occasionally on a show. Many times I've been to the retirement home where my mother-in-law lived, leading singalongs for the elderly residents.

The 5-string banjo is used in two musical art forms developed in America, known as bluegrass and old-time. In bluegrass, personified by Earl Scruggs, the banjo player—using picks on two fingers and thumb—plucks out eighth notes at lightning speed, creating exciting tunes like "Foggy Mountain Breakdown" from the movie *Bonnie and Clyde*. I played that style (albeit very much more slowly and crudely) at those folk masses years ago, but I haven't had a pick on my fingers in many years.

"Old-time" is the other type of mountain music featuring the 5-string banjo. In this style of playing, picks are not used. Instead, the old-time banjo player uses his or her fingernails to pluck down on the lower strings and the ball of the thumb to pluck up on the little fifth string, as he sets the timing of the tune for the fiddle player. Plunk, plinka, plunk, plinka, and so on. While playing this way, the shape of the right hand is like a claw and there's not much relative motion between the fingers, so the style is known as "clawhammer." I enjoy this clawhammer, or "frailing" style of playing very much. It's surprisingly forgiving of arthritic fingers and wrists like mine.

Aficionados of "old-time" will get together in somebody's home for a "jam" in mid-morning, and bring their instruments and some food and drink and stay all day and well into the night. My only problem with bluegrass and old-time music is that many of the tunes don't have lyrics and even if they do, the players usually don't sing them. And the fact is that as much as I love the banjo, I use it primarily to get people singing. So, I alternate the frailing style of Grandpa Jones—depending on the song—

with a type of strum I've developed over the years that lets me involve the fifth string and add little rolls as I play alongside the words to the song.

Barbershop-type singalong songs from the gay 90s and roaring 20s featured 4-string banjos with a vastly different sound from the 5-string. If there's anything original or unique about my playing, it's that I love to do those kinds of songs with the 5-string banjo. I don't know if it sounds good, but it certainly sounds different. And the folks at the retirement center seem to love it, those being the tunes they remember and love.

Let me close this ode to the banjo with a question: Do you know the greatest audience a home-body, banjo-plunkin' old-timer can have? It's five or six little grandkids dancing in the kitchen to the music while Grandma's laughing and trying to cook. I could play for them all night.

Once Upon a Time, College Presidents Did It All

As I made the decision to retire from Georgia Tech, I reflected on my father and recalled that he was the reason I had come to Tech in the first place. He had gone off to college there a long time ago, and had never stopped talking about how the experience had altered his life for the better.

Chambless Wilberne McGill graduated from Tech in 1928, four years after hitchhiking to Atlanta from Parrott, Ga., with a cardboard suitcase and four dollars in his pocket. When he matriculated he was already 21, having alternated years going to high school with his brother Ray while the other brother helped their father all year with the family farm.

Cham's last ride had dropped him off right in front of the administration building—The Tech Tower, the only original building still standing today. Now in the middle of Atlanta, the thriving Southern city known as "The City Too Busy to Hate," Tech was then on the outskirts of town.

He entered the largest building he had ever seen and encountered a lone secretary.

"May I assist you, young man?"

"I hope so. I am looking for President Marion Luther Brittain."

To Cham's surprise, he was told, "He's in his office, right through there. Go right in." He did so, and was greeted warmly by the executive.

"Ah, yes, Mr. McGill. I have your letter. Says here you want to attend Tech to further your education."

"Yes sir, I do."

"Well, your high school grades and recommendations are splendid, and I'm pleased to admit you as a Yellow Jacket. Is there anything you need?"

"Yes sir, I need three things—a loan, a room, and a job. I think I can handle the rest."

What happened next was the ultimate in service, a tale that Cham would retell a thousand times over the next 70 years.

President Brittain made three phone calls. The first was to the Vice President of a bank, from whom a loan was granted to Chambless, sight unseen.

The second call was to a kindly woman on Techwood nearby, who ran a boarding house and who had a room with board available, and yes, on President Brittain's say-so, would "let it" to Chambless. The third call was to the publisher of the Atlanta Constitution, and presto—just like that, the new freshman had a job. His three pressing needs having been met, his college career was off to a great start.

Years later, I told that story to my buddy Rosita Jackson Smith, who broke into laughter. I told her I had always thought it was a fine, touching story, but not a *funny* one, so what was she laughing at?

"Come on, Dave, don't you see? You've just proved that back then, the President was also in charge of Admissions, Financial Aid, Housing, and Career Services. Now, we have a director and four or five assistants for each!" And I had to agree that yes, that *was* funny.

My friend Wayne Clough, the President of Georgia Tech at this writing and himself twice a Tech grad, loves the above story. There are indeed a lot more people under him in the Tech Tower today, such as Executive Assistants, the Provost, vice provosts, associate vice provosts, and so forth, before you even reach the heads of departments like admissions, financial aid, housing, and career services.

Dr. Clough's job today is very different from that of the presidents of long ago, but he does share one thing in common with them: As did President Brittain with my father, Dr. Clough loves to meet and talk with the students.

The Old Stump Puller's New Home

The F.J.J. Sloat Dredging Company was owned by two brothers, Joe and John Sloat, whom everyone knew by the monikers "Cap'n Joe" and "Cap'n John" because of the fleet of dredge boats and tugboats they owned and managed out of the office in Slidell, Louisiana.

When the Cap'ns were in their 70s, their health began to decline. By that time their children were grown, married and scattered, with none of them having any interest whatsoever in taking over the business.

So, having given a half-year's notice to the employees, there came a day when the dredges, tugs, machine shop and office equipment, and the land and building had all been sold, and—for the last time—Cap'n Joe and Cap'n John and my dad, who was their accountant, just locked the doors, mailed the new owner the key, and drove home across Bayou Bonfouca for the last time.

I have such fond memories of those two kind men, their company, and the site. Cap'n Joe and Cap'n John hired me in my high-school summers; my pay was 90¢ an hour, which I think was minimum wage in those years in the 50s. I painted signs, helped with the payroll and accounting, and ran errands in an old truck that you had to shift with a lever that came up out of the floorboard.

Sometimes I would drive the truck to get parts for the machinist, Harry Galatas, and I liked to watch him work whenever I could. To lift the massive engines into position to work on them, he would use a huge chain hoist, also known as a come-along, or a "stump-puller." The ease with which Harry could move that heavy machinery around fascinated me, and I'm sure my observations played a role in my ending up in the field of engineering mechanics years later.

About the time they closed up shop for good at Sloat's, I was on my way back to the South with my degree and my family from the University of Kansas, to take up a teaching/research career at Georgia Tech. We stopped in Slidell for a few days en route.

I found my dad a little sad about the demise of the company that had been his vocation for well over twenty years. I told him how much it had meant to me personally, how I knew I would never have a problem handling money because of all the times I had made the books balance; how I became a good and careful driver hauling equipment around; and how, with a laugh, if all else failed, I could always paint signs for a living.

Then I said, "I wish I had written and asked for something from the company to remember it by." I was thinking of a ruler, maybe, or a paperweight, something bearing the logo of the F.J.J. Sloat Dredging Company, but Dad surprised me with his response:

"How would you like to have Harry's old stump puller?"

"Whoa, Dad, you have that thing? It must weigh 200 pounds."

"Yep, it's in the shed, if you want it."

I did want it. I had visions of impressing the neighbors with it whenever something big needed moving. Plus, I was just starting a career in mechanics, and what better symbol of my hard-earned expertise than a gigantic stump-puller?

Somehow Dad and I got the thing into the trunk, and we probably gave the auto's springs a hernia but we got the stump puller to Atlanta and I wrestled it into the little workshop in the basement.

And there it sat for 35 years, waiting for the stump that never materialized.

In my most recent effort to clear out and clean up, I reluctantly decided to let the stump-puller go. They said on the phone that they'd take it at Goodwill, but when I drove it to their van, the manager was there. She overruled the worker who had told me to bring it in, on the grounds that the sort of person who would use it wasn't likely to shop in their stores.

Next I called the one and only logging company in the Yellow Pages. They unceremoniously told me, "We don't pull stumps no more. We jis knock 'em over and haul 'em out with tractors and backhoes and stuff."

Then a machinery company turned it down, saying they wouldn't be able to get liability coverage on equipment that old.

By this time, I was getting worried and thinking I might not be able to give away the treasured tool and, if not, what in the heck was I going to do with it?

I needed to find someone who would appreciate the stump-puller for the workmanship, someone with respect for fine old tools. And on the very next call, I hit the jackpot. Don Lawson, who owns a landscaping and grading company, sounded interested and said, "Tell me where you live, and I'll come see what you got."

Don took one look at Sloat's old Yale-Townes stump-puller and said, "I don't know if I'll ever need to lift anything big enough to use it, but I'll take it just to hang on the wall of my shop. Be a great conversation piece."

We loaded it on Don's pickup, and I had a wistful look on my face as I thought of my dad, the Sloat brothers, and their company which had fed, clothed and sheltered our family through all those years of my youth.

I felt better as Don drove away, though, because he stuck his head out of the window, smiled and said, "Yore old stump puller's done found itself a real good home."

The Prince of Coincidence

It's too bad the Guinness Book of World Records has no entry for the greatest or the most coincidences, because if it did, I think I'd be listed in there. Coincidences follow me around like that little cloud that constantly hovered over the character Joe Btfstlk in the great comic strip of yesteryear, "L'il Abner."

For example, one Sunday night in my working days I was working on a technical problem and was looking for an equation I needed. It took a while, but finally I found it, and its number was (11.11)—It was Equation 11 in Chapter 11 of the book. Something seemed puzzling about that number, and then it dawned on me that it was also the date—it was November 11th. As if that weren't enough, I glanced at the digital clock, and—you guessed it—it was 11:11 p.m. I should've dashed out and found a poker game, because surely that night I'd have been dealt four aces. The next day, I made a purchase at a store, and when the cashier rang up the bill, it was $11.11.

Another day in June of 1990, I was discussing a research problem with Bob Bless, one of my graduate students who had just become a father. We were debating whether the data for a computer model we had developed should include 28 or 29 layers of optical fiber. As Bob was leaving, I wished him a happy first Father's Day on the upcoming weekend. He thanked me and returned the good wishes and asked, "Come Sunday, how many Father's Days will you have enjoyed?"

I was unable to say whether the answer was 28 or 29, because our oldest child was born June 20, and I didn't recall whether he was born before or after Father's Day back in 1962. Bob said, "Hey, those are the same two numbers we couldn't decide on for the past half-hour. Man, that is *weird!*" But not to me; Bob didn't know he was working for The Prince of Coincidence.

One of the multitude of coincidences I've experienced is an ongoing one. After my mother died in 1993, I went through a sad period. Then one day, I was sitting in a booth in Junior's Grill, on the Georgia Tech campus. I looked out the window, and saw on the brick wall of the French Building its street number in large numerals: 237. There was something familiar about that number, but I couldn't place it. I sat there staring, and I thought of my mother. I didn't seem able to stop looking at the number or thinking of my mom, and I wondered what it could mean.

That night, I was driving home, and I turned onto Piedmont Road, and there on a sign was its highway number: 237, the same number, and again without trying I thought of my mother. Before I got home, I had remembered what was special about 237. It was our telephone number when I was growing up in a small town in Louisiana. The operator would say, "Number, please," and if I was calling mom I would answer, "237," and the operator would make the connection. I remember saying aloud in the truck, "Are you saying hello to me, Mom?" I truly believe that she was, and continues to, because since that day, I'll bet I've noticed the magic number 1,000 times in my daily tasks. One day the stock market dropped 237 points, another day a sports article said if two baseball players made the Hall of Fame as expected, the membership would grow to 237. Yesterday in the shower, I looked at the Denorex shampoo bottle and it contained 237 ml. And today, a car in front of me had license plate #237-MLL. And on and on.

My father died two years after my mother. In going through Dad's house, I came across an old combination lock box. Shaking it, I could hear papers inside, but I had no clue what the combination was. Then into my mind flashed a smiling image of my mother. I smiled back and knew what I had to do. I moved the dial to 2-3-7, and bingo, Open Sesame! They had set the combination to their phone number, way back in the 1940s. Nothing of monetary value was in the lock box, but it was yet another memorable moment.

And now I want to tell you the true story of the origin of The Cat-Ranch Letter, which is simultaneously the tale of my biggest coincidence.

In 1965, while I was in graduate school in engineering mechanics at The University of Kansas, a friend named Will Jorgensen received a copy of a funny letter from his dad in California. The letter had originally been written by one Barry Crabbe, on bogus-looking stationery bearing the letterhead of "Hong Kong Importers" on Canal Street at the Mississippi River in New Orleans, Louisiana.

The greeting of the letter was "Dear Buster and Lou"; it is important to remember that, for it will demonstrate to you shortly (a) how small the world is; and (b) how some people have no shame.

I made myself a copy of the letter, and filed it away somewhere. A year later I graduated and Carolyn and I and our two children moved back to the Sunny South, to settle in Atlanta, Georgia. Twenty years later, going through some old papers, I one day came across my faded old mimeographed copy of The Cat-Ranch Letter. That night, I was going to a barbershop harmony rehearsal, so I stuck it in my pocket to read to my friends afterward.

After the meeting, some of us went to a bar to have a beer, sing some more songs, and tell a few jokes. During a pause, I thought of the letter and took it out of my pocket, and announcing to the buddy sitting next to me that I had something of importance to share with him about a sure-thing investment, I began to read.

I had hardly gotten past the first sentence when my friend, Larry Crabbe, interrupted loudly, "WHOA!!! Where on Earth did you get that, Dave? Let me see that!" And he snatched the letter from my hands, read a few lines, looked up at me, and said, "This is unbelievable."

Well, to make a long story a wee bit shorter, the letter had originally been sent to Larry (whose boyhood family nickname had been "Buster," after the cowboy star Buster Crabbe) and his brother Lou in Atlanta. Their brother Barry had written and mailed it about 26 years previously, and, it being so funny, copies had proliferated and traveled around the country. Barry really did work at The Hong Kong Importers in New Orleans.

Here, now, is how small the world is: out of a quarter of a *billion* people living in this country, the very first time I read it to one of them—after 20 years and over a thousand miles distant from where I'd obtained it—*I was reading it to the person to whom it was originally addressed*. Now *that* is a world-class coincidence.

Some time later, I saw the Cat Ranch Letter once again. Someone had mailed it to *The National Review* as if it were his own creation, and had received undeserved accolades when they printed his stolen story. (As a testament to the letter, however, a quarter-century later not one word had been changed.) Another time, after I gave a Toastmasters speech about the Cat Ranch Letter, a friend in the audience sent me yet another plagiarism, this one having been pilfered and mailed to *The San Francisco Chronicle*. Some people have no shame.

Anyhow, I'll bet by now that I've whetted your appetite for the letter itself. Here is Barry Crabbe's masterpiece:

"Dear Buster and Lou,

I don't know if you would be interested in this, but I thought I would mention it to you because it could be a real 'sleeper' in making a lot of money with very little investment.

A group of us are considering investing in a large cat ranch near Laredo, Mexico. It is our purpose to start rather small, with about one million cats. Each cat averages about 12 kittens a year; skins can be sold for about 20 cents for the white ones and up to 40 cents for the black. This will give us 12 million cat skins per year to sell at an average price of around 32 cents, making our revenue about $3 million a year. This averages out to about $10 thousand a day, excluding Sundays and holidays.

A good Mexican cat man can skin about 50 cats per day at a wage of $3.15 a day. It will only take 663 men to operate the ranch, so the profit would be over $8,200 per day.

Now, the cats would be fed on rats exclusively. Rats multiply four times as fast as cats. We would start a rat ranch right adjacent to our cat farm. If we start with a million rats, we will have four rats per cat each day. The rats will be fed on the carcasses of the cats that we skin. This will give each rat a quarter of a cat. You can see by this that the business is a clean operation, self-supporting and fully automatic throughout. The cats will eat the rats and the rats will eat the cats and we will get the skins.

Eventually, it is our hope to cross the cats with snakes, for then they will skin themselves twice a year. This will save labor costs of skinning, as well as giving us two skins for one cat.

Sincerely,
Barry Crabbe"

Reunion Remarks

I went to high school in Slidell, Louisiana, and graduated in 1957. Since then, our class of 44 has had two reunions—the 21st and the 40th. We started in the 19th year getting ready for our first reunion in the 20th year, but it took two years in the planning, hence the first was the "21st." In the months leading up to the second reunion, I was asked as valedictorian to prepare some remarks for the dinner gathering:

Dear Graduates, Spouses and Friends of the Class of '57:

Carol asked me to prepare a few words. She said Ancil would be talking about our school years together, so would I please come up with something about us outside those 12 years. I think she had in mind what has happened to us *since* high school, but that has been covered extremely well in the reunion booklet she and Jackie, Janith and Johnnie so kindly and laboriously put together for us. It remains, then, for me to talk about the only other years we have lived on this earth—the first six years of our lives, years that led to our formation as a very special group of boys and girls who met and grew up together and then went our separate ways to become successful men and women.

I really have only one point to make, which is that it was the unique time in history during which we were little children that, more than anything else, made us the good people that we are. Most of us were born in 1939. Hitler had been on the move for some years by then, but that was the year of his brutal attack on Poland, the start of a World War that was to last six more years, the formative years for us classmates.

During those years we all had someone in the U.S. military effort that got prayed for every night. I had four uncles, three in the Army (one a medic in Patton's army) and one in the Air Force. My wife Carolyn had an uncle in the Army, another in the Navy, and her Godmother was an Army nurse, all overseas. So we were well-grounded in the need for—and the power of—prayer.

We learned the meaning of the word "scarce" as soon as we could talk. We had to conserve *everything*. I had to eat everything on my plate, and as a result there is no food on earth that I won't eat, to this day. We watched our parents turn out lights and recycle some things and fix others, and ration items such as gasoline. Teamwork and doing things for others was instilled in us much more deeply than it is today, in large measure because of what the free world was enduring and desperately attempting to overcome.

We received excellent training in the hunger for news. I can recall my parents devouring the paper each morning and huddled by the radio at night to find out how the war was progressing. And I recall vividly when the war ended, that summer of 1945 when we were to begin first grade in less than a month. Our neighborhood, on the south side of town, had a huge party and Dottie Steele's dad, "Mr. George," cooked steaks for everybody. There was literally—literally—dancing in the streets. I'm sure Dottie, here tonight as Mrs. Lynn Fandal, remembers that celebration.

To sum up, we really couldn't miss in life—in an overall values sense—because of the world events that transpired during those first six years before we came together and became friends. It's wonderful to see you all again.

Prosper to Prosper

Carolyn's and my oldest grandchild is our son Michael's daughter, who has the given names Vivian Prosper and goes by Prosper. The name grew on me as I came to realize that it means, of course, "Do well in your life."

When he learned the name of his first great-granddaughter, Carolyn's dad C.J. recalled the same name somewhere back in his family tree, and he began doing genealogy research to find it. He discovered that Prosper's gggggggrandfather (six "greats") had the name Prosper Casimir Barbin de Bellevue. I'm sure he pronounced his name "Pross-PEAR", but the spelling is the same. He lived in France and was born in 1740, exactly 250 years before our granddaughter.

C.J. made her a family tree on a large poster board and titled it "Prosper to Prosper — The Road to Prosperity", which is a true work of art. The line from Prosper to Prosper spans eight generations, and along the way crosses from France to the New World.

If you go back one generation, you have $2^1 = 2$ forebears, your parents. Two generations and you have $2^2 = 4$, your grandparents. So at the eighth generation back, each of us has $2^8 = 256$ ancestors. I am proud to be one of Prosper's 256 progenitors, because "The Second Coming of Prosper" is a wonderful young lady.

Carolyn and I took her to Washington, D.C., the summer before she entered high school. We must've set a record for the most museums and monuments visited in four days. It was a grand trip that ended all too soon.

My Best Friend Honey

(Eulogy for Vivian Gertrude Johnson Mayeux,
given at her Memorial Mass, November 12, 2004)

I'm Dave McGill, Vivian's son-in-law. Our family shares with all of you the loss of a very dear person, as we at the same time celebrate her magnificent life spent here on Earth for nearly 90 years, and her entry into eternity with God.

As her life progressed, Vivian was in succession a happy child, a fun-loving teenager, a dedicated nurse, and a loving wife and mother and grandmother and great-grandmother. To all these grandchildren she was known as "Honey," preferring that appellation to words that sounded old to her like "Grandma." She moved through her ninety years of life gracefully, and made everyone feel special. If you were Vivian's friend, you could do no wrong, and after spending time with her you always felt encouraged by an optimistic, faithful friend.

Vivian was always very comfortable with who she was. She was a prayerful person who loved nature. In her last five years, at KingsBridge Retirement Center, she loved to sit on her little porch with her morning coffee and say her prayers while watching the birds and squirrels in the oak trees. She was just as comfortable with such solitude as she was with people, and she lived her simple faith rather than talking about it. As the saying goes, she never knew a stranger, and had the lifelong ability to put people at ease and listen to them. I will exaggerate a bit when I say that Honey never knew a yesterday or a tomorrow. That's not to say she didn't cherish memories or look forward to the future, but I've never known anyone who lived with more excitement in, and for, the present moment. And indeed, she told me many times, "I've always been happy wherever I've lived."

And where she lived to begin with was on a small farm on a country road in Marksville, Louisiana, where she was born on Jan. 29, 1915 on a very cold day for the birth of such a warm person. As a child, she grew up without indoor plumbing, attended school in a one-room schoolhouse, and traveled several miles to Mass on Sundays by means of a horse and buggy.

Living through 85% of the 20th Century, she experienced the advent of indoor plumbing, the automobile, telephone, gas heat, phonograph, airplane travel, air conditioning, television, computers, VCRs, microwaves and space travel. She marveled at it all, but with her humble origins could've done just as well without any of it—with the exception, she said, of the indoor plumbing. Whenever we took her back to her roots, she loved to walk on the levee of the Red River, very close to the farmhouse of her youth where a nephew and his family live today and a niece's husband raises cattle on the land.

After high school Vivian went to nursing school in Houston and worked there for a while after graduation. Proud of her Scotch-Irish heritage, she married her high school sweetheart, a Frenchman named C.J. Mayeux, in 1938. C.J.'s brothers Marvin and Bill tell stories about how painfully shy the young couple was when they were courting. Vivian came to town one day and when she passed C.J.'s house and hailed a "Hello, there" to him in the yard, he was so taken with her that he uttered the immortal words, "Fancy you meeting here!" And the first time Vivian came to dinner with C.J.'s family, she was so nervous that all she could ingest was a 7-Up.

The happy couple more than overcame their shyness, however, and began their life together in Bogalusa, LA, where C.J. was a paper mill plant engineer. Their children, Carolyn and Gayle, were born and raised there. Vivian was a devoted wife and a loving mother to her beloved daughters.

Following a job transfer to St. Francisville, LA in 1958, Vivian experienced the great tragedy of her life when Gayle died in 1960 at 19 in an automobile accident. Following Carolyn's wedding the next year, C.J. and Vivian picked up stakes and accepted transfers to Oregon and then California. During all these years, she volunteered in many ways in her various churches and communities.

After retiring from the paper industry, C.J. started a second career in real estate in Florida. During their years in Naples and on the West Coast, they loved to travel, and went to Europe, Canada, Mexico, Costa Rica, and all the beautiful areas of the United States. They retired to Georgia in 1990, where C.J. developed Alzheimer's disease in 1994 and died in 1999. Just after that Vivian moved to Kingsbridge Retirement Center, and was very happy there for the last five years of her life—with the exception of the first month, when she said several times (at age 84) that she wanted to return to her old apartment because "There's nobody here but *old people!*"

Besides family and friends, Vivian loved to do fun things. She took a ride on a nephew's new motorcycle at age 85, on that same country road of her youth, now paved and named Johnson Road. Her four great loves were writing, dancing, tennis, and bridge. She had a story published when she was 85 and played tennis well into her eighties. She was in four bridge groups right up to her final trip to the hospital. And she loved to win, *while the game was in progress*. But after it was over, she was just as happy if her opponent won. There again, it was for her the enjoyment of the present moment that counted.

An example of the hundreds of lives she touched was a young physician's assistant who had known Vivian at Post Park Apartments and noticed her name on the hospital's patient list during those last days. She came by Vivian's room to thank her for teaching her to play tennis, and to tell her she had gone on to become really good at the game.

Vivian had one habit that not many people knew about: For over eighty years, she stood on her head every morning for a few minutes. She said it was good for her brain, and when at age 85 in 2000 she told her new doctor about it and asked if she should continue, Dr. Ravry looked at her in astonishment and said, "Mrs. Mayeux, with your health I wouldn't change a thing." Honey cherished an e-mail her Marine Captain grandson-in-law Kevin sent her from Iraq. He was encouraging her after back and pacemaker surgeries and closed with the words, "Well, Honey, take care of yourself and I'm sure you'll be back standing on your head in no time." Indeed, it occurred to me that if we could all be as kind to others as Vivian was, it would indeed stand the whole *world* on its head for the better.

Honey had no regrets and looked forward eagerly to her final journey. In their daily phone conversation—every morning at 9 a.m.—she often told Carolyn, in her last months of failing health, about how ready she was to move on. And when the time came, Vivian loved the manner in which she slipped slowly away in her final days, with a lot of time spent with her three grandchildren—Michael, Gayle, and Meghan, her sister Mae, her friends John and Frances, her niece Beth, with Carolyn and me and Gayle's husband David, and with her oldest great-grandchild, Vivian Prosper (whose mom, Marianne, brought her to the hospital so she could say goodbye and play her violin for Honey right there in the hospital room).

I myself had the great joy of knowing Vivian for 44 years, the last half of her long life. I met her when her daughter Carolyn brought me home to meet her parents in St. Francisville, Louisiana in 1960. It took a while for me to become close to C.J., but Vivian and I hit it off immediately, and as she reminded me a few days before she died, we never had a cross word. Surely not many men can say that one of their best friends in life was their mother-in-law, but I can. Vivian taught me many things, including patience, the art of listening, and the game of bridge. I enjoyed playing bridge in one of Honey's groups every Wednesday, after which we would retire to her porch for a drink and a chat. I will cherish the memory of those conversations. Once she recited a funny poem for me about a fly and a flea that flew up a flue. I wish I had written it down, because now it's lost forever.

When Vivian was starting to slip into a coma (out of which she was to step into Heaven two days later), I found myself alone with her for a few minutes. I spoke to her, even though I didn't think she could any longer hear me, let alone respond. I thanked her for all that she had done for me all those years and especially I thanked her for her surviving daughter, my wife. She surprised me yet again by opening her eyes and saying softly, "I'm so glad you two found each other."

Honey liked old, simple tunes learned from her uncles Tom and Pat who played fiddle and guitar when she was a little girl. One of those songs contained 15 words that described what one always felt in the presence of Vivian Johnson Mayeux: "Where seldom was heard a discouraging word, and the skies were not cloudy all day."

We will miss her very much until we see her again on the other side.

The Vivian Mayeux Memorial Bridge Group

After Biggs died, his widow (my mother-in-law), Vivian, was becoming acclimated to her retirement community at Kingsbridge, but she missed her bridge friends and their weekly game very much. Two of them were able to drive to Kingsbridge once a week to play, so Vivian called me.

"Dave, have you ever played bridge?"

"Not once in my life, Honey."

"Well, I know you enjoy games. What card games have you played?"

"Let's see, other than games with the kids like Go Fish, Battle, Spit, Crazy Eights, and so on, a long time ago I played a lot of Hearts, Bouré, and Canasta. Why do you ask?"

"Because two of my Post Apartment friends are going to come over here once a week and resume our bridge group, and we'd like you to join us. And since you've played Bouré, you definitely know what a trump is, and we can teach you the rest. How about it?"

That got me started five years ago. They did indeed teach me to play, and I've been driving over there every Wednesday ever since.

I love the game, but even more than that I love the people I have met. Two of the originals—Mary Ellen and Vivian—have died, and the other, Frances, can no longer play because she is having trouble seeing and hearing. But as members of what we call The Vivian Mayeux Memorial Bridge Group pass on, we choose a new member from a waiting list and go right on playing.

I've met about 25 nice people who have substituted over the five years. Many of them are approaching the age of 90. I have to push one of our current members to the bridge room in her wheelchair, and another (a WWII bomber pilot) has Parkinson's and it takes him a long time to walk to the room. I have to shuffle the cards for him and the third member because of their arthritis. But their minds and senses of humor are very sharp and I always bring something away from my time with them. Most often, it's being thankful for friends and for what I have.

Vivian's group is the highlight of my week. I think she's proud that I've kept the game going.

Becoming Gerry Atric

Drawing cartoons has been a part of my life ever since I was five years old and my Uncle George Malarcher taught me to draw several of the characters from the "funny papers," which was what we called the comics section of the newspaper back then.

It remains one of my earliest memories: a little kindergarten kid sitting there with a pencil in my hand beside the uncle we all loved, suddenly able to create some of the same images as appeared in the newspaper every day. "Amazement" doesn't begin to describe the way I felt.

At age 13 I began to work part-time as a reporter and cartoonist for the local paper, *The Slidell-St. Tammany Times*. I drew all sorts of sports cartoons based on the Slidell High teams, and later on did the same for the Baton Rouge *Morning Advocate* after I graduated from high school and matriculated at L.S.U. in 1957. Both schools had the same mascot, so I became very adept at drawing tigers. In addition, in both high school and college I would earn spending money by attending and writing up high school football games for those papers and the New Orleans *Times-Picayune* on Friday nights.

My bosses at the *Advocate*, Bud and Jim, were always trying to get me to make my L.S.U. Tiger more comical and loveable, but I never did. I wanted it to be ferocious, especially since we were in the middle of the school's famous 1958 National Championship season. I still have a sketch that Jim made of his humorous version of the mascot, and it interestingly looks exactly like the tiger of later years in the comic strip "Calvin and Hobbes."

Bud and Jim always called me "Dave" (I had been David growing up) and Jim suggested that I sign my cartoons Dave McGill because it sounded less formal. I started doing that in honor of my Grandpa, Dave Dill, so if it were important, I could go back through the scrapbooks and get close to the exact date when I appropriated my nickname.

I drew cartoons of all types for the college papers at L.S.U., the University of Kansas, and Georgia Tech (*The Reveille, The Daily Kansan,* and *The Technique,* respectively), and for the *Lawrence* (Kansas) *Journal-World*. I also had a few published in the *Times-Picayune* and *The Atlanta Journal-Constitution*. And for a number of years I drew editorial cartoons and wrote a weekly column for *The Georgia Bulletin*.

I became interested in caricatures along the way, and drew them of children in pastel chalk at church carnivals. For many years I drew a caricature of the rector at Cursillo weekend retreats. These would be signed by all the team members and presented to the rector at the end of the event. On one of the Cursillos I was the rector myself, and the team surprised me with a caricature by the artist Stan Rouse, a friend of long standing. I have told Stan several times the true statement that "I got the best caricature of them all." It hangs in my basement office.

The only "rector caricature" that ever brought a tear to my eye as I rendered it was one I did of a young man I didn't know. He and his wife had taken in a three-generational family of Vietnamese immigrants for an extended period. I depicted him leading the family off of a Vietnamese fishing boat onto the shores of America.

The most fun in my cartooning avocation was in portraying comical incidents that occurred in my family or in the lives of friends. Some of those get brought out and laughed at as much as 40 years later.

All of the above paragraphs have set the stage for the title of this story. I found through the years that editorial and sports and family cartoons tend to write themselves, but what is truly difficult is coming up with something funny every day or every week. So my own Holy Grail in cartooning was the comic strip, something I had thought about, off and on, ever since Uncle George's little lesson.

I tried four times over the years to syndicate comic strips, always failing. I had a tall stack of rejection letters until I realized one day how depressing it was even for a pack rat to keep a bunch of responses each of which said, albeit in nice language, "NO!"

The last of the strips was entitled "Gerry Atric." It featured a 101-year-old man of that name who helped his single-parent granddaughter raise her children. He was patterned in appearance after Carolyn's dad, the immortal "Biggs." I came close on landing Gerry with the syndicates, but in the end it was the same old "no." One editor told me he liked it but thought it was a bit ahead of its time.

Disagreeing, I decided to try to syndicate it myself on a weekly basis. That proved to be somewhat of a success, as I had Gerry in 14 papers across the sun belt at its zenith. I finally stopped drawing it 20 years ago and moved on to other hobbies, but I think I could do a much better job now with Gerry, what with my arthritis et al. Maybe it was ahead of its time, after all. I am now *becoming* my creation!

See what you think. Here are six of the strips.

I once asked some friends at a weekly church group to say a prayer for the success of the comic strip I was trying to sell.

Jerry McCarthy, one of the members, piped up and said, "Dave, would you please bring some of the cartoons to the meeting next week so we can see how hard we have to pray?"

The "Gerry Atric" strip about Gayle's pajamas (on the facing page) is the only one that actually occurred in the real world. The original cartoon is hanging in Gayle's home, reminding her of how busy she was as a child.

To order additional copies of

The Prince of Coincidence

visit

www.unitedwriterspress.com

Write Dave McGill at

**3753 Gladney Drive
Chamblee, Georgia 30341**

He'd love to hear from you!